SWIMMING WITH SALMON

Roderick Shaw

HEDDON PUBLISHING

First edition published in 2021 by Heddon Publishing.

Copyright © Roderick Shaw 2021, all rights reserved.

No part of this book may be reproduced, adapted, stored in a retrieval system or transmitted by any means, electronic, photocopying, or otherwise without prior permission of the author.

ISBN 978-1-913166-40-3

Cover design by Roderick Shaw.

Although the author, translator and publisher have made every effort to ensure that the information in this book was correct at press time, the author and publisher do not assume and hereby disclaim any liability to any party for any loss, damage, or disruption caused by errors or omissions, whether such errors or omissions result from negligence, accident, or any other cause.

www.heddonpublishing.com
www.facebook.com/heddonpublishing
@PublishHeddon

Dedicated to daughters Kirstie, Sadie, Badger, granddaughter Sofie, and to life-long friends.

About the Author

Roderick Shaw is a painter who has diversified into writing. This is his second book.

He was an illustrator in London, with regular work from BBC TV and other freelance work, before entering advertising with J. Walter Thompsons. Rod worked with a number of other agencies and was Art Director with Y&R until he returned to his native Shropshire.

These bite size snippets scan a timescale from the 1940s to the 1960s, recording deeds and misdeeds in post war Britain: from choir to juvenile court; from art college to life in London. Families tended to support each other, and life-long friendships were formed.

We had a full house: two grandads, one grandmother, a mother, a father, two brothers, and during the war a conscientious objector in the attic. So guidance and support was readily on hand and mine was a family I felt privileged to be part of. My mother dished out discipline but it was always deserved. Whenever it was needed, she was one hundred per cent behind me.

www.roderickshaw.co.uk

Grinner, Bob, Pal, Tex and the author

Swimming with salmon	1
Tempting red apples	21
Watch out, Smiler's about	30
Oh, for the wings of a dove	47
Vacating the Devil's Chair	59
Playing with fire	67
Pecky's long trousers	78
The Big Bang at 71	89
The ins and outs of art college	95
Oh Carole!	105
Elephant mountain	107
Thumbs up for France	118
Adjusting to the smoke	136
The winter of discontent	140
A month in the mountains	155
A long climb and a missing German	162
The Driving Test	167

Swimming with salmon

Grubby knees, like a battlefield, every scar telling a story. He wore grey patched shorts and a sun-faded tartan shirt. Nine-year-old Grinner rattled the letterbox on our front door. His nickname was either born from his grin, or the first four letters of his surname. Grindley. None of us knew and we didn't much care. He was just one of our mates. Grinner. One of the gang.

Grinner lived across the street from our house, with his mother, brother Trevor, and later his father, who had been a prisoner of war. Grinner, Pecky (who lived three doors away from our house) and I had been friends since we were five-year-olds.

Pal Weston was another important member of our exclusive group, as one of his married brothers Ron had a garden which ran down to the river, in a perfect spot for fishing. Pal was the youngest of a family of five. We were always welcome at his house. His lorry-driving dad, Tom, had permanent laugh lines, literally, and he was always ready for a joke.

Grinner's one sock was uncomfortably rucked up under his instep, while the progress of the other had been arrested by a hole which had caught on his heel. The top of the hole peered over the back of his left shoe, like a rising moon; a common sight in those days, when socks were darned or left with a hole.

This was another one of those long, hot summer days that seemed to stretch to forever. The sun bounced off the pavement and warmed the brickwork of our house. It was the start of the school holidays in about 1948, I think, and the sun seemed to shine all summer long.

The day was buzzing with promise. Grinner had a loose bundle, clamped under his arm to stop it falling apart. Inside the green towel was his bathing cozzie. He shuffled impatiently, stood up close to the glass panel, then stood back and squinted.

The sun shone, heating his back. Dog-like, Grinner cocked his head to one side, looking for the tell-tale shadows through the patterned glass, of someone about to answer his call. He was never one for being patient.

'Come on, bloody hell, hurry up,' he thought. He fiddled about in his back pocket and felt the reassuring weight of his jack knife. In the fluff at the bottom of his side pocket, he found a couple of mangled sweet coupons. 'Great,' he thought, 'I'll pop into Grimshaws' and get a slab of Bluebird toffee.'

Inside, I ran down the hall, opened the door and shouted to Grinner, "Might see you later, my mum said I canner come swimming just because I have stitches in my leg. But I'm working on her."

***

The day before, I had smashed a minnow jam-jar trap on a rock on the edge of the Rea Brook, leaving me holding the string attached to the rim of the jar with fierce jagged glass shards. Now useless as a minnow trap, I had swung what was left of the jar in a circular clockwise motion, building up momentum before letting it go to smash against the railway bridge opposite.

I'd felt a dull sting and looked down to see a gaping pink gash in my right calf and blood weeping down my leg, staining my sock. Pecky said, "I'll go and get you a towel or you could bleed to death."

He and Grinner squeezed through the rusty galvanised fence behind the garages and disappeared at speed, dodging the traffic on the main road, and up Whitehall Street. The two of them hot-footed it, panic stricken, to number 17, my house.

On arrival at my home, Pecky stretched up on tiptoes and pulled the knob of the spring-loaded doorbell, sending loud peels reverberating down the tiled hallway. He and Grinner took an apprehensive step back from the door, fearing my granddad would answer.

Pecky's panic must have clouded his judgement, as the big bell was rarely pulled; once it was, there was no stopping it until the coiled spring had unwound and run its course.

My grandad, George Henry, an ex-RSM who was not over-fond of junior bell ringers, was disturbed by the ringing. Unrolling his massive frame from his armchair, he lumbered out of the living room and down the hall, adjusting his braces on his way to the front door.

His bulk spilling out of his waistcoat, he filled the narrow hallway, blocking out the light. George Henry cast a large, ominous storm cloud, fragmented by the patterned glass.

All imposing six-foot-one of my grandad towered over Pecky and Grinner, as he asked in deep, sonorous tones, "And what can I do for you two?"

They both quivered and Pecky nervously gabbled, "It's your Rod, he's cut his leg, real bad, Mr Peacock."

Grinner echoed, "Yes it's real bad cut, we need a towel or summat."

Grandad muttered, "Silly young bugger," and grumbled back down the hall.

At this point, Grannie Peacock came down the hallway, white with panic spreading across her lined face. Gran was a five-foot bundle of kindness. She said, "Where is he?"

"He's down by the railway bridge on the Potts, Mrs Peacock."

As they were deciding what to do, I appeared at the bottom of the road, heroically limping up towards the house. I had removed my sock and tied it around the wound, in an attempt to stem the flow of blood. It sort of worked, although aesthetically it left a lot to be desired.

Granny Peacock nearly passed out on seeing the gory dressing. Grandad Peacock, with a grave look, said, "That's going to need stitches."

Gran ushered me into the living room and put a towel on an armchair. Seating me on it, she bathed the wound with warm water and spread some iodine on a clean piece of bed sheet, torn to make a bandage. The sting from the iodine made me wince.

My father drove me up to the Royal Salop Infirmary and we sat in a large, impersonal waiting room. It was full of people, mostly children with arms in slings, or bloody bandages on limbs, some with bare feet and one with a home-made arrow in his shoulder.

When it was our turn, the doctor took off my makeshift bandage and looked at the wound. "Ah," he said, "that's a good clean cut." He bathed it and cleaned up my leg. Then he froze it and inserted six stitches, closing the gap and applying a pale pink square plastic plaster. "Off you go," he said, "and keep it clean."

***

At the door, Grinner said, "Mossy, Tex, Bob and Pecky have already gone down, they'll be there by now. Oh yeah, and the salmon are jumping. See you later then, so long!" was his parting shot as he ran down the street and disappeared around the corner by Mr Morris's, the Abbey Gardens park attendant's house.

Mr Morris was a real old grumble guts. He revelled in being miserable and always did his best to spread that misery on all, including his wife. He carried a stick, not to steady himself but more as a weapon against us.

His wife was the complete opposite. She was a happy, tiny mouse-like person, who tried her best to compensate for her husband. She would call us and pass sweets or biscuits down from a little side window, out of sight of Misery Guts. She was kindness personified.

I grabbed my swimming costume and a towel and walked into the cool, dark interior of our living room. My mother Ada was laying down the law. "No swimming for you, me lad," she said with authority, "so you can put that bathing costume back on the line."

"But Mum!"

I went no further. The look etched on her face said it all.

After the hospital, I'd been taken home, where my mother, returning from work, gave me a real dressing-down for being stupid and scaring my granny half to death.

But that was yesterday. Surely by now the incident was

history. Forgotten. I was fighting fit and raring to go.

The only reminder was the large pink plaster, and a slight numbness in my lower leg. I peeled back the edge of the plaster and looked at the stitches. 'No blood, no problem,' I thought. 'I feel great.' I took my swimming costume off the line in the kitchen again and walked into the living room.

"Put those trunks back on the line, now!" my mother ordered.

"What trunks?"

"The ones you've got tucked inside your shirt."

My mother was firm and emphatic, without being loud, but there was little doubt she meant what she was saying. Based on experience, I knew there was no point arguing and no amount of persuasion or mini tantrums would weaken her resolve. Perhaps this disciplined approach and her height of six foot was why she quickly made Sergeant in the wartime ATS. But on a warm sunny day which held so much promise, I had no choice but to continue arguing my case.

"But Mum, all the lads have gone. I will be careful. I won't be late, I won't leave my socks behind like last time – honest I'll just…"

"No, you won't, because you're not going. Right," she dictated.

I twisted my face into what I thought was an appealing sort of sad look. I even tried to summon up some tears and said, "I didn't mean to scare Gran." But my mother's face was set in stone and it gradually dawned on me that my pleas were all to no avail.

'Even a top barrister or the Gestapo wouldn't shift her,' I thought. 'And didn't the doctor tell you to keep it clean, use your loaf!'

Underneath, I knew she loved me, which was why she was

blocking my freedom. However, I wished sometimes she didn't love me so much. Today was such a day.

After Grinner's departure for the weir, I sat on the leatherette settee in our living room, fingering a hole I had made two Christmases ago with a bow and arrow. It had been part of a Robin Hood outfit; a Christmas present from Uncle Tom. It comprised a cardboard target propped up against the settee. This didn't stop the arrows which I had fired at it. Only Uncle Tom could get away with buying me such a present as he was my mum's favourite brother.

Pretending to be absorbed in my comic, I devised a plan to get my cozzie back off the line in the kitchen and make my escape to join the lads at the weir. After what I thought was an adequate passage of time, but in fact was little more than a minute, I put my plan into operation. First, I went upstairs to the bathroom, where I opened the window that faced the back garden.

I put the lid down on the toilet, which was just under the window.

Then I bounded back downstairs into the living room. I plonked myself into the chair, picked up the *Beano*, and pretended to read.

My mother kept half an eye on me, looking over her glasses as she darned a large hole in a blue sock stretched over a wooden mushroom.

I got to my feet and slipped into the kitchen, closing the living room door behind me. I took my bathing costume off the indoor line and rearranged the remaining laundry to disguise the missing item.

I stuffed my cozzie into my shirt and casually walked out of the back door, moving out of sight around the back of the house. The open bathroom window presented an easy target and, having crumpled my bathing trunks into a tight ball, I took aim and got it right first time. Bull's eye! My trunks sailed through the open window into the bathroom, landing on the toilet seat. Now it was essential to get back through the house and upstairs before somebody used the toilet.

"You are a fidget, what are you up to now?" my mother asked as I walked through the living room.

"Just going to the bog," I said.

"Why didn't you use the outside toilet?"

"I didn't want one then, and there was no paper."

Once in the bathroom, I quickly dropped my shorts, took off my underpants and replaced them with my swimming trunks, before pulling my shorts back on and hiding my underpants down the back of the boiler in the airing cupboard.

I grabbed the scruffiest towel I could find in the bottom of the airing cupboard and hurried along the landing. I listened, then tiptoed down the stairs, avoiding the fourth step from the bottom, which had a built-in creak.

I shouted through the living room door, "Ta ra, see you later!" I ran down the hall and out into the sunshine before my mother could question me, or Grandad George Henry could rise from his chair. Slamming the door behind me, I sprinted down the street and out of sight, around the corner into Hollywell Street. The day was hot. The sky clear-blue right down to the horizon. By now, the lads would be enjoying the cool waters of the weir.

I ran twenty steps, then walked ten to keep up a steady pace. It was the one thing I had learned in the Scouts, which I had joined to get one of those hats like the Canadian Mounties wear.

My time in the Scouts was cut short by a dishonourable discharge, for tying up the leader of the Wood Pigeon patrol, using knots of my own invention. He was released by the Scout Master, who didn't appreciate my personal take on knot-tying, and I never got my Mountie hat. The discipline in the Scouts didn't suit me. Awarded badges for specific activities but even though I always had a sheath knife for camping, I couldn't have the badge for this until I had my Woodman's Badge, and so on.

Soon, I was footing it under the dripping dark-grey metal railway bridge, with its studded grey girders splattered by pigeon droppings. I emerged from the dank, deep shadow of the bridge into bright sunshine and sweated my way up to the top of the hill, to the entrance to Castle Walk.

The tarmac path ran between a formal avenue of poplar trees and black metal railings down to Castle Bridge, crossing the River Severn two hundred yards upstream of the weir. I found the hole where a railing was missing and the two either side were as bowed as Mrs Grimshaw's legs (Grinner's description).

I squeezed through the gap. The field was bright green and yellow and the grass long and dewy damp, soaking my sandals and turned my feet buttercup-yellow. Great! 'No cows in the field,' I thought, 'not that I'm scared of them.' But sometimes they would follow you and if they had young they could turn nasty. Worse than a bull, sometimes.

In my eagerness to join my mates, I took several tumbles and excited dives over tussocky clumps of grass, or treading air in hidden ditches. My feet were covered in pollen and my wet legs attracted seeds like the proverbial to a blanket.

But my focus was on the roar of the water and, above that,

the squeals of my mates, and the fun I was missing. With rising enthusiasm, I reached the river and ran down to the concrete edge of the weir, shouting, "Alright, lads."

I was quickly out of my shirt and shorts. I walked out across the slippery bottom edge of the weir, where my mates were engaged in a screaming weed fight, scooping up swathes of silk weed and throwing it at each other.

On other days, we used that same silk weed as a bait for the red-finned roach that held in the current, enjoying the oxygen-rich water below the weir. When we were too idle to dig worms, we would tie silk weed onto our hooks and trot them down in the frothing current under home-made swan quill floats. They were beautiful fish, red-finned bars of silver reflecting the quality of the water.

Like our floats, our rods were all home-made – mostly seven-foot garden bamboo canes – as were the floats, which comprised a swan quill pushed through a cork with the top dipped in red paint.

Mossy's rod was a converted bow and arrow. We removed the string, painted the bow a ghastly bright gloss blue, and made runners out of the ends of safety pins. Having been a bow for so long, it had developed a permanent bend. Consequently, it looked like he had hooked a huge fish.

Some of the keener anglers in the gang managed to lay their hands on old tank aerials, with the addition of cork rings glued together, sandpapered smooth and finished with whipped on runners and a coat of varnish to finish the job.

The result was a half-decent though very heavy rod and I was the proud owner of one such weapon. I edged out across the weir on wet, slippery stones, trying not to stumble or get my plaster wet. After receiving three feet of wet silk weed, which wrapped around my shoulders, I became engaged in the ongoing fight. The turbulent water crashed and splashed up my legs. My plaster was soaked and slowly turning a tell-tale green.

"Shit," I said, looking down at my calf. "Mum will spot that and I'll be in real trouble."

Tex reassured me, "It inner that bad, mon, stick the corners back down and sponge it a bit and Bob's your uncle."

The sun by now was high and hot, reddening our shoulders and drying out the weed that was out of the water, so that it smelled and lost its sheen, and turned a dirty dull matt grey-green. There were minuscule aquatic insects in the weed, which was probably why the roach were attracted to it.

A green and white Pecky shouted, "I'm going in to get this crap off!"

Grinner complained, "I've been in, it's bloody freezing I'm not going in again."

With that, Pecky – being Pecky – dived in and went down to the pebbly bottom, and was swept downstream in seconds, like a salmon kelt returning to the sea. He bobbed up a hundred yards downstream from the weir then came back, heaving himself over the edge and shouting, "There's a few salmon down there, maybe we could catch one!"

I heard somebody say, "It's alright, it wunner be that cold."

Turning round, I saw it was Mossy. Who else? I thought. He was a total maniac

Mossy stood out from the rest of us as he went to a private school. He wore a grey suit with a badge, but worst of all his cap sported rings, which easily identified him as from the other side. However, he was happier in our company than his schoolmates' and spent most of his leisure time with our gang. Mossy didn't like being at a school which separated him from his mates and gave us an excuse to treat him badly. He was forever retrieving his school cap, satchel and school scarf from trees, other people's gardens, and wherever else we had chucked them.

But if we had problems with the Castlefields lot or the back of the sheds gang, we would shove Moss as our champion into the fight, encouraging him: "Go on Moss, kill him, he inner that tough!"

Mossy carried his bruises like trophies. He deemed it an honour to get a black eye or a bleeding nose on behalf of the rest of us. Often, he dragged himself home with mud all over his school uniform and rips in his jacket, but never a tear in his eye. We never told him as much but he was definitely one of us and a valued member of our gang.

It suited us better to let him think he had to undertake these heroics to maintain his membership of our unique set-up. He boasted a reputation for doing just about anything that required high risk and high energy and when required he was a good scrapper, although it was not really in his affable nature. This endeared him to the rest of us.

Diving into icy-cold water was tame in Mossy's book. He went in with a long plunge and bobbed up next to Pecky, who was swimming back upstream, against the current. They both swam into a backwater and pulled themselves onto the bank, then walked back to their towels. Pecky, shivering, wrapped his wet towel around his shoulders, saying, "Did you see all those salmon spinners down there, Moss?"

"Yes. Loads of Devon minnows and salmon spoons, we should go down and get some," Mossy said. "We could sell 'em to the salmon anglers and make a bloody fortune. I saw three salmon down there."

Another valued member of the gang, Tex was the Johnny Weismuller (Tarzan) of the gang; not because he was a brilliant swimmer, but because of his unique technique, which created so much splashing that it looked like he was wrestling a crocodile and the croc was winning. His front crawl was over-flamboyant, his hands entering the water in a flourish, only inches in front of his nose. There was little forward movement. It was more a case of side to side.

Tex's face always looked scrubbed clean, making the perfect backdrop for his red nose, which earned him the nickname Rudolph. Obviously, he preferred his other nickname, Tex – which we tended to use, rather than upset him.

Like Tarzan, Tex had an animal friend. Rex was a long-legged, disreputable terrier crossed with a coconut mat. A canine terrorist who could out-think, out-run and out-swim most other dogs, and a good number of adults. He was definitely, like his owner, part of the gang. His coat was rough and usually wet, and he had a permanent shiver of excitement which was enhanced when near or in water. His intelligent, hopeful brown marbled eyes followed us everywhere. Rex could do most things and followed us over fallen trees, or open railway bridges, balancing on a single line. He was an infinitely better swimmer than his master, with an exceptional talent for swimming underwater. If a brick was thrown, Rex would duck-dive beneath the surface time after time, until the brick was dragged up the muddy bank onto the grass, accompanied by incessant barking to draw attention to his achievement.

Shivering with expectation, he stood waiting for someone to throw the brick back into the water. The ends of his teeth were worn flat from his brick retrieval. Although Tex was the official owner, Rex belonged to all of us.

Mossy shouted over the roar of the water, "Rod, look over there, isn't that your dad waving?"

I exclaimed, "Shit, bloody hell, I'm for it now." I couldn't hear what Dad was shouting over the roar of the surging water, but I got the message from his wild gesticulating and pointing towards the Castle Walk bridge. I sort of understood his semaphore.

By now, the dressing was hanging off my calf by one corner, green and limp. The lads washed my leg then rubbed the Elastoplast with the wet towel and attempted sticking it back onto my leg, which was proving nigh impossible.

"Best thing," Grinner said, was to "take it off and say your leg's got better or say you took it off because it was itching"

"They wunner fall for that," I replied.

Bob, the sensible one of the group, pitched in, "You should'na have got it wet in the first place."

"Oh shurrup, Bob," Tex commented. "Bloody know all, you're a bloody big head."

Bob replied, "Well, he was daft to have gone swimming in the first place."

"I'd better shove off, see you later," I said.

When I squeezed through the railings, my dad was waiting, an impending storm etched on his face. He warned, "You're in real trouble. What the bloody hell were you thinking of? Just look at your leg."

I cringed but said nothing, although my dad had never laid a finger on me. There was only one occasion I could remember when he tried to hit me. Some weeks earlier, someone had thrown a potato through our front bedroom window. Consequently, that window was filled with a piece of cardboard for several weeks. My father was continually badgered to fix it by Mum. "It looks like a slum," she'd say over and over again. He agreed apologetically, as if he had thrown the spud in the first place.

Glass was a bit scarce in those post-war days but on a misty Monday, Dad came home triumphantly with putty and a sheet of glass cut to size.

Having fitted the pane of glass, my mum Ada was full of praise for him. He in turn bathed in the glory.

Next day, the sun was trying its best to break through thin cloud cover. The doorbell rang – my mates calling for me, waiting on the street

I ran along the dark landing with one sock on, into my parents' bedroom to let the gang know I was nearly ready and on my way. I put my foot on the windowsill and, gripping the frame of the sash window with both hands, heaved myself up so I could shout down to them.

However, my upward movement meant my knee went through the pane of glass my father had just fitted. Hearing the breaking glass, Dad came upstairs and along the landing, snorting, "Bloody hell!" and repeating it – "Bloody hell" – as he advanced towards me like a raging bull. I immediately jumped sideways, over their big double bed. My father came round the bottom of the bed as I shot under it, out of the other side and back over the top again. I repeated this several times until his anger had subsided.

When we arrived home from the weir, my mother was waiting in the living room. She believed punishment was necessary to keep me on the straight and narrow.

Secretly, I knew she was right.

She started off by saying in a grave voice, "What the hell were you thinking of? Just look at that plaster, you could catch something from the water with that open wound."

"But it inner open, Mum." I knew this would be followed by some sort of punishment.

I wasn't wrong.

She took the strap off her ATS bag, doubled it, and said, "This is going to hurt me more than it hurts you."

I suggested, "Well don't do it then."

She responded, "It's not a laughing matter."

Grannie Peacock came out of the kitchen, pleading, "Don't hurt him, I can't bear it."

Gran was always on my side and stood firmly in my corner. She was five-foot-nothing of understanding and kindness and I could do nothing wrong in her eyes.

However, Grandad Peacock revealed his RSM army background by agreeing with my mum, saying, "He's got to learn, it's all about discipline."

It didn't hurt that much but I cried out in pain as if in agony, so that she felt the punishment had been hard enough to teach me a lesson, and for me to maximise sympathy from my Gran.

In fact, I knew my mum was right and I was in the wrong.

My brother Tad agreed with my mum, commenting, "You're thick, our kid."

"Shurrup and keep your beak out," I responded.

I loved my brother but sometimes he got right up my nose.

My gran was the glue that secured peace in the family. One of her favourite sayings was 'spread your bread upon the water and it will be returned ten-fold', or something along those lines. It might have been three- or even four-fold. It was summat like that, it was out of the Bible. She had a lot of snippets like that from her bible.

Years later, that particular philosophy manifested itself. During the war, my mother had worked with a man from London, who was a conscientious objector. He had nowhere to stay and couldn't find any sort of accommodation. His name was John and he worked with my mother at the Pay Corp at the big sandstone hall at the top of our street. She suggested to the family that perhaps we could offer him accommodation

However, with my grandad as an ex-RSM, and my father and two uncles serving as soldiers, it was not a done deal. Granny Ada, backed by my mother, persuaded Grandad George Henry.

And so John was happy in our attic, and eventually his wife moved up from London to join him, and they stayed with us in our attic for the most of the remainder of the war.

Six years after graduating from art college, I was in London looking for freelance illustration/design work. I had some work from BBC TV and Radio Times, and after an interview with an advertising agency they suggested I try British Rail. After a phone call, I arrived at BR offices and sat opposite a kindly-looking man. I opened my folder and he looked at my work. I had a strange feeling I knew him.

"What part of the world are you from?" he enquired.

"Shrewsbury," I replied.

"I know Shrewsbury," he said. "What part are you from?"

"Cherry Orchard, Whitehall Street."

"What number?"

"Seventeen," I replied.

He exclaimed, with a look of utter surprise, "You must be little Roddy."

It was John, who had lived in our attic when I was just a toddler. So my Gran was right all those years ago, about

17

spreading your bread upon the water. Although it was me who got the benefit, not my Gran, it did result in plenty of bread at a time when I needed it.

I did not venture to the weir again until Grinner called on a wet and windy day, saying, "The salmon are jumping."
"I'll get my rod," I said, "hang on."
As I was coming through the house with my rod, Gran asked, "Where are you off to?"
"Grinner's here, we're going fishing."
With concern etched on her face she responded, "Well don't get near that river!"
When the water was at a certain height and the salmon were running, huge fish attempted to jump the weir. It was usually too deep for us to venture out onto the sill of the weir. We fished in the back water for perch, or just stood and watched the salmon attempting to clear the barrier, to continue their journey upstream to their spawning redds.
Mossy turned up with his permanently bent royal blue bow/rod. Other kids, seeing the bend in the rod, would shout, "He's got a good fish on there!"
"I'd love to get one of those on my hook," Mossy enthused.
"It'ud pull you in," Grinner observed. "Anyway, you need a fly rod or some spinners. They wunner take a maggot, but they may take a worm."
We three stood mesmerised. One fish leapt up and thumped down on the side of the weir, a full-finned acrobat. It landed on the concrete edge out of the water, nearest to me.
I quickly dived on it and attempted to wrestle it up onto the grass. It was like trying to hold on to a slippery muscled youth and the salmon escaped and tumbled, flapping,

broadside down the weir, back into the churning depths below.

In the summer months when swimming below the weir, we sometime came in contact with salmon, but never came close enough to grab one.

"It was a hen fish," I said.

Tex asked, "How do you know it was a female?"

"Easy, it's like humans," I said. "It was prettier. The males have bigger heads and a projecting lower jaw."

"Dunner be daft, how do you work that out?" Tex said.

"I've seen pictures and female fish have the edge."

A mate at school told me of a lad he knew in Wales, who wired salmon with a strand taken from a rabbit snare attached to his wrist. With his wire noose, he would slide it over the salmon's head and tighten it behind its gills. Tragedy struck on an August day, when he attempted wiring a fish in low water. He missed the salmon and wired a tree root by accident. He couldn't release the noose from his wrist, or the noose which tightened around the tree root or his arm. The next day, rescue services found the boy's body still attached to the tree. Naturally, whether this story was true or not, it put us off trying this particular method – although we used it on trout from the safety of the banks on side feeder streams, with some success.

So we satisfied ourselves by watching these magnificent bars of silver making their journey upstream to Wales and the redds to spawn. They had overcome so many dangers from nets, seals, fishermen and weirs, to lay their eggs. In one way, I was glad I didn't hold onto that fish. By now, it would be skirting around Shrewsbury and I felt happy and wished it well on its fantastic journey from the north Atlantic to the headwaters of the Severn, to help produce the next generation of salmon.

Many anglers fished close to the bottom of the weir, where the fish congregated, jockeying for position ready to make their leaps. Eventually, the powers-that-be outlawed fishing too close to the weir, to give the fish a better chance of progressing upstream to the spawning gravels.

Poetry in motion protected.

Tempting red apples

Throughout its length, from its source in the Shropshire hills to the confluence with the River Severn in Shrewsbury, the Rea Brook was one of our favourite stamping grounds. In common with moorhens, flashing kingfishers, cormorants and a variety of ducks from mallards to goosanders, we spent a lot of our time in and around it.

Brown trout thrived and could be seen in the evenings, making big, lazy circles as they rose to sip flies from the surface. In the hot summers, indolent chub lay midstream, seeking oxygen and picking off food from the current, with minimum movement.

Everywhere, there were eels, which we caught with our homemade rods, or sometimes with night lines. I often set as many as six lines a night. They comprised cheap sea fishing line threaded through a round piece of lead pipe (the outlet pipes on our house had got shorter over time and my dad eventually noticed that there was only a couple of inches of one pipe sticking out of the wall), then a matchstick, then more line, down to an eel hook. The matchstick allowed the eel to pull the line with no resistance but, pulled in the opposite direction, the matchstick engaged and played its part. The lines were secured in the bank with hammered-in stakes, which were hidden in bankside vegetation.

Near to the Abbey Church, under a railway bridge, was an ancient, walled stretch of deep water, which held a large head of perch. We fished for them, using minnows as bait.

These minnows were captured by dipping our hands into the holes in the surface of Shrewsbury Weir, then placed into large jars. We used home-made swan quills and cork floats with the end dipped in red gloss paint. We trotted these crude floats downstream under the railway bridge to great effect.

On a cloudy, humid day in early July, I jumped down from the wall at the back of the cottages in Brook Road, landing in the long dew-soaked grass. I ran excitedly alongside the brook, up to a massive conker tree a hundred yards upstream.

The tree was our major meeting point; a refuge, and our headquarters. It had huge nails as climbing aids up to the first branches. From there, it was easy climbing to safety in the crown of the tree, where we had fixed a couple of short lengths of scaffold planks to form a platform.

This gave us a good vantage point to see up and down the fields and the Potts Line. A huge haulage rope swing, with several big knots on the end, hung close to the brook's edge, midway between the tree and the brook.

Some of the gang were there, sitting in the grass. Grinner sat astride the knot on the end of the rope. He swung gently in and out over the brook, looking down at the grass, dreaming.

As lads, we thrived on adventure, always living life to the full; always looking for a dare, and always in the best of company.

Grinner asked, "Seen Mossy lately?"

"No, I ain't seen him today," I replied.

At this point, as if by magic, Mossy arrived, dragging a length of thick lorry rope and enthusing, "Look at this, lads."

Tex – faithful Rex as always by his side – said, "What is it?"

Grinner chipped in, "It's a bloody rope, you dozy prat."

Tex responded, "I can see that, you stupid bugger, but what's it for? Why has it got half a house brick and hooks on the end?"

Mossy, holding up his rope and hooks, explained, "It's for dragging the brook." He beat a path through the heavy vegetation, willow herb, nettles and dock leaves, down to the edge of the brook.

Pecky said, "I'll do the chucking." Higher up the bank, Grinner and I stood on the rope.

Swinging it back and forth to build up momentum, Pecky let it go and it landed two-thirds of the way across the brook, with a mighty splash. He let the rope settle and sink, then started to pull it back. It hadn't moved far when its progress was arrested, coming to a sudden halt. It had hooked on to something and was stuck solid.

Bob warned, "What if it's a body?"

They all heaved and strained on the rope. Huge clouds of mud coloured the brook for thirty yards downstream. A gurgling, slurping sound bubbled up and out it popped. Some of the lads fell over as the mystery object was spewed up from its muddy grave. They dragged it out through the reeds, cussing and swearing as it flattened the bankside vegetation, until they had it on the bank.

"It's a motorbike," Tex enthused.

Rex the dog was barking encouragement as they pushed the bike along the bank upstream to the 'cow drink', a shallow part of the brook where cattle had eroded an open bay so they could get down to the water to quench their thirst and cool off.

We took our shoes and socks off and pushed the bike into midstream, where there was a reasonable flow.

There we began to wash off the clinging mud by cupping our hands and chucking water over the bike, poking it with sticks to clear the wheels.

A man walked across the field. It was Corona Jones, walking his poodle, whose barks were totally ignored by Rex, who was more interested in the bike.

Corona shouted, "What you got there, lads?" He was called Corona because he drove the Corona float. His float was always a welcome sight when he rattled up the street with precious cargo. Grinner always said, "He's got the best job in the world, he can drink as much Corona as he likes."

"It's a motorbike, Mr Jones," shouted Mossy.

Once clean, we pushed the bike up a small hillock.

"Right," said Pecky. "Who's going to do the test flight?"

Bob sensibly observed, "It won't bloody fly."

"No, I know that, you dumbo," Pecky answered. "You wait and see it go off the bank, though. You'll see it fly, and a splash-landing."

Grinner said, "Anyway, whose rope is it, and who put the brick and hook on the end?"

"Mossy. It stands to reason," Tex added.

The rest of us agreed it was Mossy's responsibility.

With no objection, Mossy triumphantly sat astride the bike, on what was left of the saddle. Just a metal skeleton remained.

Ready for the test flight, a proud smile spread across his face. With Pecky on one side, Grinner on the other, and Tex and I bringing up the rear, we ran at speed and pushed Mossy over the grassy edge. The bike immediately picked up speed, in what was a bumpy, bone-rattling ride. Mossy took off like a stunt rider and flew into the air, culminating in a massive explosion of water. He disappeared underwater. Then he bobbed up.

He triumphantly shouted, "That was fantastic! Who's next?" as he pushed his steed to the top of the bank, sporting a tear in his trousers thanks to the skeleton saddle.

All present, having witnessed Mossy's ride, displayed a complete lack of interest.

Tex summed it up by saying, "I inner bloody daft."

"You mean it's an act?" Pecky quipped.

"Cheeky prat," Tex said.

Mossy was always the fearless one, who would accept any challenge, and we all basked in the reflected glories of his escapades. His aim was to be totally accepted by the rest of us non-private-school types. Like a mini-Ulysses, he accepted challenge after challenge.

On another scorching hot summer's day in early July, Mossy again came looking for the rest of us. When he caught up, he was on one side of the brook and we on the other.

He shouted, "Alright lads, how did you get over there?"

Pecky responded, "We all jumped."

"Never!" Mossy exclaimed.

"We did, didn't we, lads?" A chorus of agreement rang out.
"But we did it separately, not all together."

"There's no way you can jump that far," Mossy asserted.

Grinner explained, "It's like an optical illusion, 'cause the bank's higher on your side, it inner as far as it looks, you'll be really surprised."

Mossy walked off to the other side of the field, until he almost disappeared out of sight in the long, dry, waist-high, hay fever-inducing grass. He scraped his foot, raising a dust cloud, like a Spanish bull preparing to charge the matador.

Tex said, "You're right, he will be surprised."

Mossy sort of snorted and came like an express train in a cloud of dust and thistledown, attempting a leap that even the great Jesse Owens in his prime couldn't have achieved.

It was a valiant effort but he hit mid-stream with an explosion of water. Rex the dog jumped in and joined in the excitement.

Mossy stood up. We all doubled up with laughter and Mossy, being Mossy, joined in as he waded out to retrieve his school cap, which was floating downstream into deeper water.

He shouted, laughing as he went, "Great, wunner it?"

We built a fire on a shingle beach and hung Mossy's school jacket on a branch, wringing out his socks and shirt and doing our best to dry them out in the heat. Mossy looked on in his underpants. Bob dried Mossy's school cap on a makeshift toasting fork, which he held out towards the flames. This proved very successful until he dropped it into the ash at the side of the fire. It had to be washed in the brook again.

As the fire roared and crackled, we fed it with bigger and bigger branches, until there was a base of hot grey ash. Mossy stood with his back to the fire, steaming but happy to be in the starring role and in the best of company.

Rex was still diving, barking, shivering on long, skinny legs and trying to retrieve a brick we had thrown in earlier.

When the fire had virtually burnt out, Mossy began to shiver as spots of rain could be felt, even though the sun was shining. We called another eventful day to an end and walked downstream, up Brook Road and out onto Abbey Foregate. Mossy, smelling like a smoked kipper, was damp but not soaking wet as he had been. Rex, still full of canine energy as always, bounded around us.

As we came out onto the Abbey Foregate, the sub postmaster Mr Cook greeted us, "Alright lads, and what have you been up to?"

"Nothing, Mr Cook," we chorused. "Honest."

I had utter respect for Mr Cook, as some years earlier I had squirted my water pistol down the slot of his stamp machine at his sub-post office ruining rolls of stamps inside. He and my father had sorted it out between them, without informing the police. Dad had to pay for the damaged stamps and I had a telling off from him and the strap from my mum. After that, as a matter of honour I also stopped scrumping Mr Cook's apple trees and made sure the lads followed suit.

Summers were often spent swimming and, if we were hungry, a bit of scrumping: apples, plums, pears, and even sprouts eaten raw. But never in Mr Cook's garden, even though he had the deepest, reddest apples you have ever seen.

There was one other garden where the apples shone; shiny red beacons of temptation, the sort Adam couldn't resist in the Garden of Eden. Bob observed that the tree was a bit too close to the house. To reach it, we had to get over a small side stream and over a spiked railing.

Tex, Grinner, Pecky, Moss and I crossed over the stream on a fallen tree. The fence didn't provide much of a barrier. Once in the garden, we moved up towards our goal, through a well-kept vegetable patch.

Grinner said, "Bob was right, it's a bit close."

"There's no bugger about," said Pecky.

My bright idea was for me to climb the tree, harvest the

apples, and drop them down to my mates below. I climbed up and began dropping some beauties down to the lads, who ringed the trunk of the tree. I was in full flow, dropping apples and looking down as they fielded the bounty. But the next time I looked down, none of my mates were there and the base of the tree was deserted.

I turned my attention towards the house and saw an angry, red-faced, fat and puffing man, closing in on me as I made my bid for escape. When I dropped from the lower branches, he grabbed me. "Got you! You're in real trouble now. What's your name?"

I stayed silent, which wasn't a ploy, just fear, as I had been well and truly collared.

The man marched me up to the house and into a lean-to greenhouse at the side. He stepped inside the kitchen and I heard him dialling the police and telling them he had caught me. I tiptoed to the door of the greenhouse, quietly edged it open, and ran down the garden with the man screaming, "Come back, you little bastard!"

Although he wasn't gaining on me, I could feel his red-hot rage on my back.

I scaled the fence, jumped into the small stream, waded across and ran down to where the lads were waiting at the conker tree. They sat on the bank, biting into the juicy loot.

Bob moaned, "I told you it was too near the house."

"You buggers soon bunked off."

If a copper had come looking for us, we would have soon been detected. Evidence of our scrumping was obvious, carrying on the brook downstream from the conker tree. Lovely red apples - just like Tex's nose, Pecky said. We tended to bite into the bright red part of the apple and sling the rest in the brook.

Pointing out that the man had rung the police, I said, "We'd better bugger off home."

Pecky said, "They wunner send a copper out over a few apples."

"Yes. But that bugger who nabbed me, he wunner forget my face, will he?"

"Were you scared when he rang the police?" Bob asked.

"Nah," I lied. "I knew I could get away, and he was too fat to catch me."

We all dispersed, bar Pecky. We left him sitting at the base of the conker tree, chomping on a rosy-red apple, the remaining evidence of our forbidden fruit bobbing up and down, disappearing under the railway bridge on a journey to the Severn and on to Bristol.

When Grandad saw the three shiny red apples I had brought home, he quizzed me, "Where did you get those beauties?"

"Out of Pete's dad's garden," I lied.

I gave him one to silence him and in my mind make him an accomplice; a receiver.

Grandad took out his penknife and sliced up the apple. "Lovely," he enthused. "Maybe he'd give us a few more." He reminded me of the Victoria plums I had given him last year. "See if he'll give us a few of those, too."

"I canner I lied Granddad, he's chopped the tree down, 'cause it had some terrible illness."

"Shame," he grumbled, "they were proper eating plums, they were."

He never knew he had eaten stolen property.

Watch out, Smiler's about

Smiler was our local red-faced bobby and he had a marked influence on our early lives as he tried his best to keep us in line. He was strict but fair and usually on our side.

We called him Smiler because he imbued happiness and he most times had a smile on his mottled, weather-beaten face. He was both an enemy and a friend and we all respected him on both counts, fearing and liking him at the same time.

In a group of rundown houses called Horse Fair, in the shadow of the Abbey Church, lived a woman we knew. She had deep ginger tousled Celtic hair, which was massively dense and curly. Her name was Edwards and she often shouted to us, "Hello boys, what you up to?"

She was very large and usually sported flowery frocks and equally flowery aprons, and somehow nothing matched.

I was in the company of my older brother Tad and his mates when Mrs Edwards greeted us, saying, "Boys, can you do me a favour?"

I stood in the background as Mrs Edwards handed over a shopping list of vegetables she wanted. She told us she had an allotment behind the Shrewsbury Town football ground, the Gay Meadow. "It's the one in the far corner, nearest to the station and the river. There's two shillings in it for you."

We set off with a basket she supplied.

We were scanning the rows, filling the basket according to

the list: two cabbages, six onions, some spring onions and some new potatoes, when a tall, pale man arrived. He sported a moustache and long, Edwardian sideburns.

"What the bloody hell do you lot think you're doing?" he growled.

"Mrs Edwards sent us," said Tad.

"Who the bloody hell is Mrs Edwards?"

"Well, she's the woman who owns this allotment," Jim Dales, who lived at the top of our street, tried to explain, "and she asked us to get her some vegetables. Show him the list, Tad."

"Not possible, lad, this is my allotment."

Two weeks later, Smiler turned up at our house with his sergeant, to ask a few questions. My brother showed him the shopping list, which was in Mrs Edwards' handwriting. They agreed it was evidence.

Smiler turned to me and asked, "And what about you?"

I put on my pathetic look and whispered, "I only took a onion and I've ate it."

"Well, I think we can discount you from our enquiries."

The sergeant nodded his approval and I left my brother and his mates to face the music. In fact, we were all spared an appearance in court. Instead, Mrs Edwards was summoned and made to pay a heavy fine. My brother kept the two shillings she had given us.

It was the end of the term, and we had we broken up for the summer holidays, looking forward to what seemed like endless days of freedom that stretched out before us. It had rained heavily overnight, big blobby raindrops hitting the windows and dribbling down the glass, swelling the drops below until the glass was awash.

In the morning, by the time I had eaten four Shredded Wheat, the sun sent shafts of optimism and everything was steamily drying out.

Grinner and Mossy knocked on my door.

"Who the hell is that now?" Grandad moaned as he made to rise from his armchair.

"It's the lads for me, I'll get it," I answered quickly.

I opened the door to the enthusiastic pair. "We're meeting Tex and Bob on the Potts Line."

The Potts Line ended in the shadow of the Abbey Church. There were warehouses where a scattering of white dust covered sheds, some of the wagons, and a lot of the men, giving them a ghostly look when dusk descended.

There was a small station but there were never any passengers. Just two rooms, a table, and a coke-fired stove, which glowed in the winter. Mostly it was locked and empty but on occasions a guardsman and sometimes drivers sat inside on the wooden benches.

Very occasionally, in the winter, a guardsman would let us into the little room. It always had a coke fire, which gave out lots of heat and smelled lovely. The guardsman would give us cups of tea in tar-stained enamel mugs. As far as we knew, his name was Joe, but we addressed him as Sir. He would sit by the open door of the stove, cleaning his pipe with an old penknife. We rarely saw him actually smoke it.

Joe had constant stubble on the lower half of his brown, ruddy face. He was a kindly man and when he was eating his sandwiches he would pull a whole Spanish onion from his bag. "Want a slice of onion, lads?" Then with his penknife he would cut us a slice each and we enjoyed the onion, even though it was stained red from the rust on his penknife blade.

On odd occasions, he would let us ride in the guard's van up as far as Hook-a-ate village.

Leaving my house, Mossy, Grinner and I walked down three houses and knocked on Pecky's door. Pecky's sister Jennifer answered. "He's up the garden with his jackdaw. I'll give him a shout."

"Who, the jackdaw?" Grinner joked.

Pecky had picked up the jackdaw when it was a young, flightless bird. He looked after it so well it had become tame and got used to Pecky handling it. He called it Jackie Peck – Jack for short – and reckoned he was teaching Jack to talk.

Pecky shouted, "Come in, Rod, and see Jack."

We piled in and Mrs Peck as always greeted us, "Hello, lads."

Dave stood in the doorway with Jack perched on his wrist. The bird was a handsome fellow, with a cheeky look, shiny blue-black plumage, and a wicked glint in his eye. Jack took off and flew in a circle around the kitchen, with Mrs Peck shouting, "Get that bloody bird out of here! Look what it's done!"

Jack had shat on the plates drying on the draining board. Pecky took his feathered friend and put him in his cage in the back yard.

"Let's go, lads," Pecky said as he put Jack back in his cage. The three of us set off to the Potts Line, crossing Abbey Foregate, down through the cottages in Brook Road and scraping through a gap in the rust-tinged corrugated fence by the railway bridge. Here, we were met by Bob and Tex, and of course the four-legged Rex, who greeted us, jumping up, demanding attention. The five of us looked towards the little station to see if anyone was watching us. We crossed two tracks and dodged under the wagons and onto the blindside, where we couldn't be seen by the few railway workers and the warehouse men.

We climbed up into one of the wagons, only to find the tarpaulin full of rainwater. We tried three more wagons only to find a similar story. Rex was down on the tracks, under the wagons, barking furiously.

Pecky said, "Sort that bloody dog out, Tex, he's drawing attention to us."

We decided if we were to enjoy the comforts of the tarpaulin retreat, we had to get rid of the water, Pecky and Grinner using the spike on their jack knives which is supposed to clean horses' hooves. They stabbed the tarpaulin until it resembled a colander and the water drained away so we could sit and talk.

Meanwhile, Tex had picked up Rex and climbed halfway up the side of the wagon, as far as he could get, with Rex affectionately licking his face, which didn't help. Two of us leaned over the edge of the wagon and I got my hand through Rex's collar while Pecky got him by the scruff of the neck. Tex pushed from below and we heaved the quivering mass of coconut matting onto the wagon. Rex flopped out on the canvas, trying to lick us in gratitude.

In a siding adjacent to a deserted, white-dusted warehouse, we settled down in comfort, the tarpaulin like a giant hammock, well out of sight of railwaymen and the men from the builder's merchants.

We pulled out our catapults to compare them. All the forks had been cut from trees and came in various sizes. The pouches were fashioned from leather tongues cut from our shoes. Most of my shoes were devoid of tongues; I tended to only wear dark socks so Mum wouldn't detect I was tongueless.

The catapults were quite effective weapons and we had acquired a degree of expertise, especially when we used ball bearings. We tested our weapons by firing into the large timber yard adjacent to the Potts, arguing with each other as to which had gone the furthest, watching our stones bouncing from log to log in this graveyard of massive tree trunks.

Our attention turned to the warehouses ten yards away. Most of the windows had been smashed. So we came up with a method of testing the catapults' firing power on the windows on our side of the warehouse. The idea was to see if the stones would carry through to the other side of the building.

With every tinkle of glass, Rex excitedly barked his approval.

Bob being Bob pointed out that the dog's barking may attract attention. He wasn't wrong.

Tex shouted, "Let's scram, there's Buster Jones!"

We all chorused, "Who's Buster Jones?"

"He lives by me and he's a bit of a bugger."

As one, we all got over the side of the wagon as Buster bawled, "Come here, you little bastards!"

Using the ropes that secured the tarpaulin, we soon hit the deck. Rex got thrown into a trackside bush to soften his landing and we all got away, slithering down the embankment, through the wire fence, and into the comparative safety of the timber yard.

We looked back and could see Buster and another workman, both in white dust-covered overalls, as though they had dived into a sack of flour. Eventually, they gave up.

We sauntered back down the line and out of sight. Rex was whining, scratching furiously and growling as he dug huge holes.

"Bet there are rats in there," Tex observed, "he's a bugger for rats."

Bob said, "Shurrup, I can hear voices."

Grinner climbed up a stack of sawn planks so he could see the open space where the lorries parked and turned. "It's your bloody mate Buster," he moaned, "and he's with a bloke from the timber yard, he's bloody ratted on us."

Tex chipped in, "I told you Rex knew there was a rat about, and Buster inner my mate, thank you very much. I'll smash you one if you say he's my mate."

"Well you know him, dunner you?" Grinner responded.

"Yeah but that dunner mean to say he's my mate, I hate the bugger. I know Charlie Tipton from the back of the sheds gang and I canner stand him, so shut your gob."

Grinner said, "Yes, Charlie's looking for you, Rod. He got hit on the ankle by a stone and he saw who threw it."

I replied, "And who was it?"

"It was you, you nit," he sneered.

"Oh shit," I realised he was right.

Rex at last put up a rat and chased it across the open space, biting it at the back of the neck and nonchalantly tossing it into the air over his shoulder.

On spotting Rex, Buster shouted, "That's their dog. They're here somewhere."

Whilst they followed Rex, we ran across the yard, between more stacks of timber and under the railway arch to safety. We stood on the bank of the Rea Brook at a place we called Ickey Bridge. Rex soon joined us, soaking wet but with no sign of Buster or the other man.

"This is a great place for eels," Pecky said. "You canner eat 'em out of there, though, too damned muddy. They just taste of mud, ask Joey. He was with me last time we fished there."

"And there's a big pike hangs around here." Pecky said. "Our Mike's seen him."

"Well if it's a big'un it's probably a female, not a Jack," Tex said.

"I know Don Gilbert's seen it an' all, he told me."

"Yes! He said it was as a big as a bloody crocodile."

We scrambled over a small wall with railings on the top and went along the lane behind some terraced houses, the last one being Tex's. He went through the back gate, saying, "See you tomorrow, lads."

The rest of us went back up Coleham Head into the Foregate. Bob peeled off by the Abbey Church and down Railway Lane. We were all soon at home after another great incident-filled summer's day.

I opened the door into the lounge, where my brother was slouched in an armchair reading the *Wizard*, his favourite comic. He looked up. "What have you been up to?"

"Nowt," I replied, "don't stick your nose in."

He threatened, "I'll give you a thick ear if you dunner watch it.".

My mother came in from the garden and embraced me, putting her face to my hair. "You smell of the open air, have you been up the brook?"

"Yes," I said, "dinner do much, though, just messed about with the lads."

That evening, Dad came in from the work at the Spitfire factory, proclaiming, "We're having chicken on Sunday."

Granddad said, "Chance'd be a fine thing."

"No, really!" Dad assured the family. "My mate's popping it round Saturday morning."

Chicken in those days was mostly eaten at Christmas and this was mid-summer. We were excited by the prospect and looking forward to Sunday.

On Saturday morning, hearing the doorbell spring into peeling chimes echoing down the hall, I ran to the door, thinking it was the lads.

When I opened the door there stood a boy about the same age and size as me. He asked, "Is this Mr Shaw's house?"

"Yes, he's me dad."

"Well it's like this. Can you tell him he canner have the chicken cause it's got better?"

On receiving the news, Grandad said, "I thought there was a bloody catch in it, why didn't he eat the chicken himself?"

"Did he think he'd die of chicken pox?" I wondered.

My mum said, "Chickens don't get chicken pox."

"Well why do they call it chicken pox then?"

Mum replied, "Go and help your gran put the sheets through the mangle."

"But Mum, what about the chicken pox?" I persisted. "If I caught it, would I be a chicken? One of the lads at school told us if you get German measles you break out in lots of tiny red swastikas, then if they turn black you die."

"Utter rubbish, don't be stupid," Mum said.

My brother added, "If you swallowed that you're bloody thick, our kid."

When the summons to appear at juvenile court dropped through our letterbox, my mum opened it, and on reading the contents she went ballistic. Dad wasn't over-pleased, either, saying, "Silly young bugger." Grandad added to my condemnation. I immediately owned up to my involvement because my Mum always knew if I was bending the truth.

I was really scared and fed up. My court appearance was scheduled for 13th November. I was due in court on my thirteenth birthday and, worst of all, it was a Friday.

My mother tore strips off me; in fact, she filled me with regret. "Why did you make holes in the tarpaulin?"

"Well, it wunner me, but it was full of water and we wanted somewhere to sit," I whined.

Granny stayed in the kitchen and Grandad sat in his chair, poking the holes in the pepper pot and salt cellar with a needle, having warmed them by the fire.

On the day of our court appearance, I walked with my mother and saw my mates waiting outside the magistrates' court in the Old Market Hall in Shrewsbury. They were all dressed up with jackets and ties; I'd never seen them as smart as this. Full of trepidation, we entered the building and went upstairs into the dusty, oak-panelled courtroom. The magistrates sat before us in a forbidding line-up: a large, older man, bulging out of his charcoal-grey shiny suit over a button-busting waistcoat.

He sported a very unfriendly disposition. His face had the look of someone about to fart or struggling to supress one. The only sign that he was human was an egg stain on his tie.

The lady was the epitome of strictness, with a pinched, unsmiling, skeletal face and an expression that looked like she had just bitten into a lemon. Her mauve twin-set with strings of white pearls decorated her bony figure.

It didn't bode well.

The third magistrate looked reasonably normal and less formal, in a sports jacket with leather patches on the elbows, and even had a trace of a smile on his face.

My mother did her best to defend us, arguing that there were few playing facilities, but without success.

The bulging one said, "When you poked holes in the

tarpaulin, you ruined sacks of cement."

Pecky said, "Well we dinner know there was cement in the wagon."

Grinner smiled nervously and the magistrate interrupted in a deep but loud, sonorous voice. "Be quiet, boy." To Grinner, he said, "This is not a laughing matter. Breaking all those windows was an act of pure vandalism."

We didn't have the chance to point out that most of the windows were already busted.

At the end of our appearance, we were all given a severe ticking-off and a substantial fine. My mother handed me the money for my fine, saying, "That's your birthday present." She took it off me and gave it to the court.

For years afterwards, every time there was trouble or vandalism in our area, the police would come knocking on the door, right up until we were in our late teens. Apart from the odd bit of scrumping, we never crossed the line again, or at least we rarely got caught.

On one occasion, Smiler caught me dropping off a wall with a shirt full of plums. He collared me and took me to the front door of the orchard's owner and made me hand over my haul.

As we walked back towards the road, he gave me a well-deserved clip around the ear, saying, "Don't do it again or I'll have to take you in."

Even when we were being well behaved, if we saw Smiler coming on his bike we'd warn, "Watch out, Smiler's coming."

Some of my schoolmates acquired Gat air guns. They were pistols where the barrels had to be pushed in to load them and when fired the centre of the barrel shot out with a hefty kick. The cowboy films had a big influence on us when it came to acquiring a gun. Let's face it, you never saw Roy Rogers sporting a catapult.

I had seen a Diana 177 air rifle in a shop on the other side of town. I often biked there and spent time admiring it. I had little chance of owning it unless I could get a job and save for it.

My brother had a paper round, which he had been doing for three years, and he knew there was a vacancy at Crawford's for a round which covered Hollywell and Underdale Road. A mate of his, Don Gilbert, who lived in Coleham, had just packed the round in and it was up for grabs.

I hotfooted it to the paper shop. "I've come about the paper round, Mr Crawford," I said.

"Good. But how did you know about the job?"

"My brother knows Don, the lad that's leaving." The deal was struck and the wage of ten shillings a week agreed.

Mr Crawford was a tall, erect man, with a trimmed black moustache and a sparkle in his eyes. His fingers were constantly black from handling newsprint. I sort of knew him as he was one of our stops for sweets on the way to school.

The following Saturday, I went with Don on his final round so I could get to know the route. It all went well, with just a few things to watch out for, like the house in Bradford Street where he warned, "There's a nasty little terrier here. If he's out, stick the paper in the gate."

We moved on with the dog behind the gate in a show of canine hysterical frustration.

"See what I mean?" Don said. "If he's in the house, make sure your hand is well back, or he'll try to grab your fingers. In fact, I'll give you a tip, but don't tell anyone. When the little bugger is inside waiting for the paper, I push it through but hold on to the end of it and wiggle it about. The little bastard goes berserk and attacks it, tearing it to shreds. This gets him into trouble with his owners, or that's the idea."

The only other warning related to a house at the end of Underdale Road. Once there, I could see the problem through the farm gate. It was a Great Dane that looked more like a donkey than a dog, and he was loose. Don undid the latch on the gate and I said, "I inner going in there with that big bugger."

Don assured me, "He wunner hurt you, honest, he's as soft as butter."

I followed Don and, sure enough, the dog proved very friendly. I wasn't in danger of being bitten; it was more likely I'd have been licked to death.

After months of saving, mostly thanks to my paper round, plus taking back empty beer bottles to retrieve the deposits at the Crown, the momentous day arrived when I had enough money for my Diana 177 air rifle.

My brother volunteered to go and buy it, as we were unsure how old you had to be and I didn't want to miss out at this stage. He came out of the shop, grinning, with the gun all wrapped up in brown paper. He said, "I got a tin of pellets an' all."

"Bloody hell, I never thought of that."

"That's my treat, as long as I can have a few shots with it."

Back home in the garden, we unwrapped the pistol and put a bean tin on the wall. Tad took aim and missed with his first shot but put a hole in the tin with his second. "It's alright, inner it, our kid?" was his parting shot.

I stayed up the garden, taking pot shots at the bean tin. As day turned to night, I went in the house and took my gun to my room. There was a full-length mirror in my parents' room so I went along the landing and stood cradling my gun, admiring my reflection. If only I'd been able to get that Mountie style hat from the Scouts.

My Dad surprised me, saying, "What are you up to and where did you get that from?" He pointed at my gun.

"It's mine," I said.

"That's not what I asked. Where did it come from?"

"Well, I bought it."

"Where did you get the money?"

"I saved for it."

"How?"

"My paper round."

"Well, just watch what you're doing with it and no shooting birds," he warned. "And I can think of better ways of spending your money."

In the company of Pecky and Grinner one cloudy dull day, I went up the brook, taking pot shots at the odd pigeon. We walked along the backs of the gardens of Abbey Foregate.

"Hey, look at that," Pecky said. "Ain't that the bloke who rang the police when he grabbed you for scrumping?"

All you could see was a large, corduroy-encased bum. "Let's shoot the bugger!" Pecky suggested.

"Piss off," I responded. "I dunna want to get into any more trouble."

Pecky and Grinner agreed, "We'd only give him a bit of a sting from this distance."

"Are you sure?" I asked.

"It wunner hurt him that much, teach the bugger a lesson."

"But we were pinching his apples," I said.

"Yes, but some of them had grubs in them."

After some persuasion, I rested my airgun against the lower branch of a tree and took aim at his gluteus maximus, pulled the trigger and shot him straight up the arse.

"Bull's Eye!" Grinner shouted as the man jumped up, screeching, more from surprise than pain.

We retreated at speed, running back down the brook to the conker tree. We climbed up to the planks and the safety of the canopy. There the three of us sat, taking pot shots at anything that came floating down the brook.

A voice from below disturbed us. "Hey, you lot up there, come down here."

We looked down and there was Smiler looking up at us. He wasn't smiling. Instead, he had his constabulary official expression look etched on his face.

Pecky said, "Hide the gun up here," just as Smiler shouted, "And bring that gun with you."

One by one, we descended into the arms of the law. Smiler said, "Give me that gun," and he took it from me, saying, "I may have to confiscate this weapon."

"Dunner take it off me, I've only just bought it," I pleaded.

"Well, you should have thought of that before you shot Mr Baker."

"Well, it was like this," Pecky interrupted. "It wunner Rod what shot him anyhow, it were me. I wunner aiming at the bloke, I was aiming at a grey squirrel sitting on a sunflower and I dinner see Mr Baker behind, it were a pure accident, honest."

After a minor riot act being read to us, Smiler said, "Do you know, I can take this gun off you, but I'll give you one last chance." He handed over my gun, saying, "On your way and I'll have a word with your dad when I see him, young Shaw."

I didn't mind him telling my dad but I was worried how my mum would react if she found out.

On quiet days, when I was on my own in the house, I used to do target practice. Sitting in my father's chair in the living room and with the door open to the kitchen, I placed a huge bar of green Lifebuoy soap in an open kitchen cupboard. Pellets would slam into the soap. The trouble occurred when Gran had a couple of pellets in her porridge, which didn't go down too well.

This was the result of two wayward shots. I was warned by my father, who said "You're this far from losing that bloody gun." He emphasised his point by indicating with his fingers. I never used the gun in the house after that and, with stinging legs from mum's bag strap, promised my whole family.

Airguns were common then and often fights using catapults and airguns would break out. On a dry but cloudy day, Grinner's brother Trevor was engaged in a gun battle with a lad from Old Coleham. They were sneaking around the garages by the car park of the bowling club, taking pot shots at each other. Grinner and the rest of us were not involved and were merely observers.

A young girl saw what was happening and when she heard a pellet hitting the corrugated iron fencing, she ran off up St Julian Friars to the junction with Wyle Cop. When she returned, she had a young constable with her.

We warned both of the combatants and Trevor's enemy quickly reacted, throwing his Gat pistol into the nettles.

Trevor got caught red-handed with his Gat. The constable took the pistol from him and waved it around, using it as a pointer to emphasise the dangers. Trevor tried to interrupt the copper, to tell him the pistol was loaded. The firing tube retracted, the constable continued gesticulating. The gun went off and the pellet hit Trevor in the eyelid in an upward trajectory. It missed his eye by a fraction but lodged itself below his eyebrow, leaving him with a blue lump just above his eye.

The young policeman went as white as a sheet and said in a breathless voice, "We'd better get you up to hospital."

Trevor said, "No, no it's ok, I'll go home and me mum will put a plaster on it." He gave the gun to Grinner and the policeman walked with Trevor up the town walls to the Eye, Ear and Throat hospital.

The copper's words certainly struck a chord with all of us, especially with the physical demonstration and the blue lump under Trevor's eyebrow. From that day on, we treated our airguns with a bit more respect, realising their potential danger. No harm was done to Trevor and because of the constable's panic, he was allowed to keep his gun and it was all hushed up.

The next time we bumped into Smiler, he informed us he had heard about our brush with the law. We all said, "That wunner us, honest. They were bigger lads than us."

"Well, just watch your step, I've got my eyes on you lot," he replied.

"Thanks, Smiler," we chorused.

He smiled and said, "It's PC Jones to you lot."

Oh, for the wings of a dove

When he was a boy, my father attained a scholarship and became a chorister/scholar with Lichfield Cathedral Choir, receiving an education and honing his voice into the bargain. Dad had inherited his voice from my grandfather, who was a fine alto, although my father was a soprano developing into a tenor.

Grandad Shaw loved to sing, occasionally in church but mostly in pubs. He never got paid; he did it for the sheer joy of singing as he let loose from beneath his beer-soaked handlebar moustache.

My mother would sometimes ask me to go and prize Grandad out of the Crown pub, which was opposite the Abbey Church. "Tell him his dinner's ready," she instructed.

I would stand in the backyard of the Crown, from where I could hear his alto voice drifting on the heavy, smoke-laden atmosphere of the aptly named Smoke Room, out into the fresh air.

I would open the backdoor of the pub and shout, "Tell Grandad Shaw his dinner's ready."

A packet of Smith's crisps would be sent out to me and he carried on singing. After just enough time to finish his pint and his song, he would emerge and greet me with a twinkle in his eye and a smile half-hidden under that luxuriant handlebar moustache, which he wiped on the sleeve of his jacket.

He would enquire, "Is your Mum cross with me, lad?" as

we walked hand-in-hand alongside the Abbey Church, cutting across one corner where the railings had been commandeered to make arms for the war effort. Seemed ironic to me.

Walking up Whitehall Street to home, the smells of Sunday roasts filled the air – usually this was beef, and those lunches were the highlight of the week.

Pecky had joined the choir at Shrewsbury Abbey and he suggested I should join him. Initially, I pooh-poohed the idea until he said, "You get paid, you know."

For company, I asked another good friend, Mossy (who lived across the road in the terrace) to join me, so we could gain moral support from each other. The church gladly accepted us as they were short of boy sopranos, most lads thinking it sissy to wear a ruff, cassock and surplice.

The whole family, apart from my brother, were pleased with my new interest – my brother shared the 'sissy' opinion.

I didn't tell them about maybe getting paid.

The three of us attended choir practice one evening a week, usually a Wednesday. Mr Stannier, the choirmaster, would bring out a small harmonium and place it in the central aisle.

We stood in front of him.

On one such evening, Mr Stannier sat at his harmonium and we rehearsed an anthem. His bald head was just visible over the instrument. A yellow and blue light from the stained glass window cast a holy pattern on his shiny head. Above each ear, he had a small amount of black hair, like double Hitler moustaches either side of his head.

Mid-note, he stood up, looking over the top of his gold-rimmed glasses and exclaiming, "Someone's flat!"

He then made us new members sing the scale and when

it came to Mossy's turn it was obvious he was the culprit. He was flat as a proverbial pancake.

Mr Stannier simply said, "I'll talk to you later, boy, go and sit in the pews."

When we left the church, Pecky and I hung around outside to find out the result of the meeting between Mossy and the choirmaster.

Mossy appeared, complaining, "What does he know about singing, anyway?"

"Well," we both agreed, "quite a lot, as it happens."

"Let's face it, Moss, you are a trifle on the flat side."

"Well, I canner help it," he said. "I did my best. Anyway, he's let me stay in the choir to make up the numbers, as long as I sing quietly. Cheeky bugger even said, better still I should mime."

And so we performed to full houses, especially at Sunday evensong. I loved the anthems, because you could really let rip as they were big, inspiring, powerful and strong.

Roy, the leading treble, started growing whiskers and then overnight his voice broke and he became a tenor. Pecky and I were given the chance to progress. Mr Stannier asked us if we would sing a duet at evensong on Sunday. When I told my family, they were over the moon.

Pecky's reaction was, "We get paid extra."

After one choir practice, we stood shoulder-to-shoulder between the choir stalls and performed in front of an exotically-hatted full house. The butcher's wife had a broad-brimmed creation reminiscent of the Lone Ranger's, with fruit. She just needed Tonto to complete the picture. Others sported feathers alongside fruit. Most of the men were in charcoal-grey made-to-measure suits from Jacksons or the fifty-shilling tailors.

When we changed in the vestry, bass Mr Bromilow and alto Tom Pearce joined the choirmaster in congratulating us, saying, "Well done boys, you did very well."

The general consensus was we were pretty good, especially according to my family and Pecky's mum, sister and brother.

Pecky and I were on ten shillings a quarter and Mossy earned zero on account of his singing. Pecky joked he was 'flat broke'.

However, Mossy became expert at miming and was teamed up with me to do a bit of altar work. The choir had a separate collection. A sort of round velvet bag was passed along the back row of the stalls, so the men could put in their offerings, then it came down to the front row. It was passed along so that the boys could make their contributions.

Now this is where Mossy and I got involved. We were at either end of the row nearest to the altar and had been instructed that from there we would walk slowly towards each other, velvet bags in hand. Then, side by side, we were to face the high altar and walk to meet the Reverend Wilkinson. He held out a silver tray and we were supposed to simply lay the velvet bags on the tray.

However, Mossy, in his desire to please the vicar, turned the bag upside-down and started shaking the coins out of the bag. The noise as metal hit metal could be heard right down the church and the coins bounced and rattled off the tray and tinkled all around the three of us.

Making the situation worse, he started trying to retrieve the wayward coins. The vicar uttered under his breath, "Leave them boy, leave them," but Mossy, determined to carry out his Christian duties, continued pursuing every last penny from all corners and dropping them back onto the vicar's tray for repeat clanging.

Reverend Wilkinson then displayed a very un-Christian demeanour and, with a face turning red with supressed rage, reiterated, "Leave them, boy, leave them," as he turned away to walk back up towards the altar.

I turned and said, "Come on, Moss."

When we got back to the safety of the choir stalls, Mossy still had a handful of coins, which he handed over to the vicar after the service.

On occasions, we were asked to assist at christenings. Pecky and I had some very profitable christenings, as the grateful parents would give us quite generous tips for our singing and often this was doubled by the grandparents.

Prior to the arrival of a christening party, the vicar asked us to take a big chipped enamel jug and fill it.

Pecky knew the drill. We went outside and in through another door, to a very small, musty boiler room. Beside the boiler was a rusty tap.

"I thought holy water would come from something a bit more special," I said.

Pecky answered this by gripping his crotch, saying, "I'm bosting for a piss."

He then lifted the enamel jug and pissed in it.

In shock, I said, "But that's supposed to be for holy water."

He justified his actions by saying, "Choir boys' piss is sort of holy, especially if you've been confirmed and God created us, dinner he? Any road, I'll chuck a bit outside and top 'er up with water."

"Dunner the Vicar say owt?" I enquired.

"He dunner know, and it warms the water for the babbie. I've baptised many a babbie."

We went back into the church and filled the font, ready for the service. I was worried because God was supposed to know everything, so he must know Pecky was pissing in the holy water.

Pecky explained, "They all say when the babbie cries it's to let out the devil, or summat like that, but I think it's because the water's too bloody cold." In an attempt to further justify his actions, he said, "You might cry if some bugger doused you in icy water."

"Yes," I responded, "but I wunner want your piss on my head."

I did think about telling Mr Stannier about the piss in the font. But as I was the only one to know about it, Pecky would have known I was the nark. Anyway, he could deny it, and he was my mate. He did have a point about warming the water and often the baby didn't cry, which sort of justified his actions as doing God's work.

About this time, I was offered a small box by another lad in the choir, who also went to our school.

He said, "Give us some sweet coupons and he's yours."

"What is it?"

"It's a fully trained performing animal."

I opened the box and there it was, the cutest little mouse you ever did see. He looked up at me with a timorous, pleading look on his frightened little face.

Sweet coupons changed hands and I proudly walked home with my new pet. I named him Mickey. Not a very imaginative title, but he seemed to like it.

I often took Mickey to church in an old domino box. He was

happy in his box, because I usually put some porridge oats and cotton wool in with him. Sometimes, I let him out of his box so he could run up and down the prayerbook shelf in the choir stalls. All the lads gave him titbits, so Mickey couldn't be described as being as poor as a church mouse. In fact, he was a picture of health, although putting on weight to look quite tubby.

Our parents and most of the congregation had the idea we were little angels. It was an accolade we ill deserved.

At Harvest Festival time, as we walked past the huge displays of copious amounts of fruit, veg and harvest loaves, some of the apples and pears ended up secreted under our surplices, beneath folded arms and an angelic demeanour.

Another of our activities was the use of paper catapults. These comprised of an elastic band stretched between index finger and thumb. They were quite accurate. The missiles we launched were lightly chewed paper, folded once over the elastic. We were well practised at firing them. Sometimes, our targets were other boy sopranos in the stalls opposite.

But our favourite target was the bald head of Tom Pearce, the male alto. When he was at full throttle, a well-aimed paper pellet would result in a sound like a constipated owl filling the church. This hoot was amplified when two paper pellets found their target at the same time.

Mr Pearce would raise angry, red-rimmed eyes from his hymn book and scan the choirboys in the front row opposite. But the concealed weapon was easily secreted and we were all capable of assuming an angelic look.

Weddings were our favourites, as tips were often the order of the day. Mr Stannier told me that a woman had heard my singing and asked if I would sing a solo in the chapel at Shrewsbury School. My response was, "It's a bit posh up there, inner it, Mr Stannier?"

"Yes, and you need to be on your best behaviour, it's a big society wedding. They are just people," he said, "and it's a great honour. Also, they'll pay you."

"Ah, that's different," I enthused.

I was given a date in December for my appearance.

On the day of my big performance, I walked through the huge iron gates at Shrewsbury School, having been dropped off by my dad. It was snowing heavily and as I walked through the snow it compacted and creaked under my tread. I headed towards the chapel in the school grounds. I had been given a spoonful of glycerine by Dad, to lubricate my throat. This was standard practice; something he had picked up during his chorister days at Lichfield Cathedral. Although I wasn't too keen on the sweet taste, it did the trick when it came to loosening the throat.

I felt nervous as I approached the chapel. It was like being behind enemy lines. A man came out to greet me. He was tall and sported a long raincoat, down below his knees. He had a shock of blond hair and a rosy complexion.

"Morning," he greeted me, "are you the chorister from the town?" His air of superiority made 'from the town' sound like an insult, as if coming from the town put you in a lower class.

To build my own self-confidence, I thought to myself, 'You've got your own choir and lots of pupils but you anner got anyone who can sing as good as me.'

Inside the chapel, I met the choirmaster and he provided me with a towel.

"There you are, boy, dry your hair."

"Thanks," I replied. My mother had given me strict instructions to be polite at all times. I was given a surplice, cassock and a ruff, and I met the mostly male voice choir, as the boys were on half-term.

The candlelit church was full of floral arrangements in huge, polished vases, and on wide-brimmed hats, much as in my usual church.

Then came the 'do you takes' and the 'I dos' and giving of troths. I never found out what the hell a troth was, only that if you got married you got one.

(Pecky, at one of the Abbey weddings, said, "You'll have to wait till you get married, then you'll find out what it is and if you want the bloody thing."

"I dunner think it will be much cop 'cause everyone who gets married gets one and they give it away.")

I stood, the organ piped up, and I sang my solo: Mendelssohn's *Oh, For The Wings of a Dove*, which I had sung in the Abbey several times before. When the rest of the choir came in, the volume of the male choristers and the rest of the choir was truly inspiring. I looked at the smiling congregation and from this I took it they liked the singing.

After the vicar said, "You may kiss the bride," it was just about over. 'Maybe the troth is like a surprise when they go away together,' I thought.

In the vestry, following the service, I took off my cassock and surplice, put on my mac, and belted up. As I was leaving the chapel, the vicar said, "The bride's mother has invited you to the reception."

I wasn't that keen, but I was starving and I thought they'd have proper posh nosh.

The vicar said, "I'm going that way so you can walk over with me."

When we entered the large hall, it was full of chattering people clinking glasses, exploding corks, and lots of laughter.

Down one side of the room was a very long table. Not, however, as long as the one which had stretched the full length of our street to celebrate Victory in Europe. I felt a bit out of place and thought Mossy would have been more at home in this sort of company.

The tables were covered in crisp, blindingly white tablecloths, and a fantastic display of food, the like of which I had never seen before.

There were whole salmon dressed in cucumber slices, with a pea for an eye, and salads and fancy pastries. The bride's mother came over and spoke to the vicar and then turned to me. "Help yourself to food, young man, you deserve it after your lovely singing. You have a remarkable voice, and here is your reward." She handed me an envelope.

I wandered along, marvelling at the food. There were big hams, sliced beef, and lots of salads, but what took my eye was a large tray of square slices of cake. Each slice was split into four: two pink and two a pale sort of yellow, surrounded by marzipan.

I tried one and they were absolutely scrummy. I also tried smoked salmon, which had never passed my lips before. I was not impressed. Too rich for my taste; I'd rather have a tin, like we had with our salad for a tea on special days. Back to the Battenberg.

The cake stand was beginning to look sort of empty so I thought I'd better go. I slipped three more of the remaining slices into a paper napkin and secreted them into my pocket.

I picked up my coat then thanked the choirmaster. The bride's mother thanked me again and, remembering what my mother had told me to say, I said, "How nice of you to ask me." Rather than "Thanks for having me," or, "Ta, it's been great." I couldn't see the difference. Load of bullshit, if you asked me.

Outside, snow was in the air as I slithered through the large metal gates. I turned left, then right, towards the toll bridge, which headed back into town. By now, the snow was tumbling in great swirling white flakes onto the previous fall. I looked over the bridge and the Severn flowed inky-black against the white surroundings of snow.

In the middle of the bridge, I stopped again, as a rising wave of sickness crept over me. With my forehead pressed against the cold, riveted metal of the bridge, I exploded.

A projectile of technicolour vomit stained the snow. I immediately went off Battenberg and was about to throw the slices from my pocket into the river. However, I thought better of it, thinking of my brother Tad and how he might appreciate them. I looked up and down the bridge and it was deserted. No one to witness the result of my greed.

The night and the temperature were dropping, as was the snow, and I quickened my pace, as by now my mother would be worrying. She did a lot of that, worrying. The snow was building underfoot, sandwiching my soles. It squeaked as it stuck to the bottom of my shoes. I blew hot air into my hands as I progressed along the town walls, over the English Bridge, and passed by the Abbey Church as the darkness deepened.

When I arrived at number 17, I kicked the outside wall to

shift the snow from my shoes, opened the door, and once inside stamped my feet on the doormat.

I opened the lounge door to the warmth of roaring fire, saying, "It's snowing again."

As expected, my mother had been worrying. "Where have you been?" she said, looking at me over her glasses.

"Shrewsbury School, singing in the chapel."

"I know that, but why so late?"

"Well, I got an invite to the reception 'cause they liked my singing."

My brother chipped in, "So you're a bit of a star then, are you, our kid? But I wunner want to sing to them snobby buggers." "Even for one of these" I said showing the ten shilling note the bride's mother had given me.

"And you wunner want to eat this cake they gave me, then. Look, I snaffled this for you."

Tad's real name was Eric but when he was born he had thick black hair and the family said he looked like a tadpole. That name stuck with him for his life.

I handed over what was left of the cake to Tad and although the Battenberg slices were in bits, he demolished them like a hungry lion and even nibbled off the bits that were stuck to the paper serviette. He agreed that there was something magical about some posh food.

That was my only foray into the privileged grounds of Shrewsbury School, until I captained a football team from Shrewsbury Wakeman College, some years later. I didn't tell my team-mates about my singing, as I suspected most of them would be of the sissy mentality, not suited to an inside forward.

But that's another story.

Vacating the Devil's Chair

The Stiperstones are a chain of jagged tors in the wild border country between Wales and England. They are the remnants of a quartzite ridge formed over 480 million years ago. One of the larger tors is known locally as the Devil's Chair. The whole area is shrouded in mystery and although the boulder-strewn ridge was the result of severe frosts in glacial times, legend has it that the devil's apron string broke as he rose from his chair, spilling the boulders which he had carried from Ireland to fill the valley between the Stiperstones and the Long Mynd.

Mists drift in from Wales, mixing with low, swirling cloud to create an atmosphere that is pregnant with ghostly expectation – which is why we were so attracted to the area.

In the summer, we had camped in the shadow of the Devil's Chair. We sat around our fire into the early hours, making up ghost stories and frightening ourselves into the bargain.

Since then, Bob had read up the facts of the legend about Anglo Saxon Shropshire Earl Wild Edric, who had enjoyed great wealth and was the lord of numerous manors. He hunted in the Forest of Clun, across the Stiperstones and the Long Mynd. Although he and his wife Godda were real people, there are many myths and legends about them.

Apparently, the ghost of Wild Edric is imprisoned in an ancient mine with all his followers and Lady Godda. The imprisonment was for making peace with William the

Conqueror. When war is threatened, it is said he appears on his horse, galloping across the wild landscape, Lady Godda behind him, her long golden hair flowing down her back. But they always return to their prison and will not be successfully released until England returns to the way it was before the Norman conquest.

"Sounds like a load of bollocks to me," Tex surmised.

Bob insisted, "I've got a book about it if you dunner believe me."

Pal, said, "Don't be bloody awkward, Tex."

One wintry Saturday, five of us had caught the bus which slithered its way from Shrewsbury to Plox Green. We slogged our way up through a scattering of snow to the top of the Stiperstones. The snow was deeper on the top and was settling in the valley ahead. A lot of it had blown off the rocky outcrops.

We all sat on a big flat rock beneath the Devil's Chair, sheltering from the wind, slurping coffee from our flasks, and eating some of our sandwiches.

As was often the case, Grinner hadn't bothered making sandwiches. Bob being Bob asked Grinner if he would like one of his.

Grinner took one and peeled back the bread, saying, "What is it?"

Bob said, "It's cheese."

"I can see that, you prat," Grinner responded, "but anner you got any pickle in your house?"

Pecky chipped in, "You're a cheeky sod, Grinner."

By now, the snow was swirling down in big flakes against a pregnant sky.

Mossy suggested, "We should press on, dunner forget it

gets dark early and there's more snow on the way."

Grinner interrupted, "Eh, can you hear bells ringing?"

Bob said, "Yes! Shurrup, let's listen."

Tex interrupted, "It's scary up here."

Bob repeated his order, "Just listen."

We all sat quietly and listened and soon discovered the source of the sound. Blades of mat grass poked through the thin covering of frozen snow. Each blade of grass had a thin covering of ice and when the wind blew in the sharp, thin air, the grass made the sound of a thousand tiny bells as the blades came into contact with each other. We all struggled back into the straps of our rucksacks and began the descent into the valley and the village of Ratlinghope.

The snow swirled and, as Wenceslas saw when he last looked out, it soon lay round about, deep and crisp and even, changing the face of the landscape.

Once down in the valley, we stopped at the Bridges Pub long enough to consume a large bowl of chips and a pint of shandy before setting off for the final leg of our journey. An assault on The Long Mynd.

Using signposts poking through the snow, we grafted our way along lanes and onto the bottom of the the Burway; a single-track road which climbs up over the high part of the Mynd, before dropping down into Church Stretton.

Bob said, "Do you know they say the Ghost of Wild Edric sometimes appears around here as a large black dog with wild, fiery eyes."

"Give over, Bob," Tex moaned, "we dunner want to meet that bugger."

Long blue shadows patterned the snow as we tried to keep in touch with the narrow road. All the little gullies and contours had filled in and the snow had changed the look of the landscape, making it difficult to recognise where exactly we were. The snow was really deep in places and at times the going was extremely difficult. We sank up to our knees.

We struggled on and although none of us said anything, we were all becoming concerned. The snow became heavier, swirling down in big flakes that stuck to our clothes and immediately froze. This gave us an extra layer of protection.

However, Pecky complained, moaning, "I can't feel my feet, they're frozen and numb."

We all had boots on, but he had come in wellies. He stumbled on but he was not happy, losing his footing and taking several tumbles into snowdrifts. It got to the point where he complained, "I can't go on, my wellies are full of snow, and I can't take another step. I canner walk, I canner feel anything."

The light and the temperature were dropping fast as we tried to help Pecky keep upright. Eventually, we could see a lone signpost sticking up like a beacon of hope from the snow and pointing toward the Glider Station.

By now, we were all wet and bedraggled and feeling miserable as the light was exiting the day and darkness swept across the snowy landscape.

Pal said, "The relief hut is round around here somewhere." He then said triumphantly, "Look it's over there," pointing into what looked like an endless white landscape.

"Yes," I said, "I can see it."

We made our way across. In fact, there were two huts: one was securely locked but the other one was open. "I think the locked one is summat to do with the grouse shooters."

Tex and Grinner, supporting Pecky, turned up, looking relieved.

Snow had drifted in through the door. Inside the hut there were some witches'-type brooms.

Bob informed us, "They're for beating out fires and they're called besoms."

"Bloody hell, Bob, you know everything."

Bob proceeded to produce a torch from his rucksack.

We swept out the snow, and sheep-droppings. There were two benches and a sort of crude table. Pecky was laid out on the table and two of us struggled to get his wellies off. There were lumps of ice inside his wellies.

Pal asked, "Any bugger got any matches?"

Bob produced a plastic pack.

Pal exclaimed, "You're a bloody star."

We broke one of the twigs off a broom for kindling and with great difficulty smashed one of the benches to build up a fire outside the door.

Using the sandwich wrappers, we soon had a fire going. We hung Pecky's socks off the door to dry out. His feet were white. Pal said we had to get his circulation going. We took it in turns rubbing and massaging his feet and lower legs. As the circulation started to return, he cried out, "Bloody hell that's bloody painful! Ow, bloody hell, Christ, shit, ouch, go easy, bugger off!"

Outside the hut, the snow had settled and a blanket of silence muffled the landscape. The sky took on the appearance of a Van Gogh starry night and the temperature continued to plummet, as we continued to take turns rubbing Pecky's legs and feeding the fire.

"How are your feet?" Bob asked Pecky.

"I can feel them, they're not all that bad, they'll be better when I get my socks on. Are they dry yet?"

Our coats had been partially dried by the fire and so, as

darkness fell, we all agreed we should make tracks down to Church Stretton. The snow had changed the geography so we had trouble locating the top of Carding Mill Valley, which would take us off the Mynd and down to safety.

The brooms which had been stripped of their twigs we took as walking aids. The moon lit our way and using Caradoc – another hill across the valley – as a guide, we managed to locate the top of Carding Mill Valley. The progress was extremely slow as we struggled, often waist-deep in snow, following the meandering of the tiny brook, which looked like a black ribbon snaking down the valley. The first part was difficult as we descended through drifted snow, but we were soon in sight of the café on the flat part of the valley, where the going was much easier. There was no sign of life, just silence and total darkness. We pressed on down the valley, eventually passing a handful of houses, and carried on towards the streetlights on the main road, which were a comforting sight.

We walked towards the centre of Church Stretton, which was deserted.

"What's the time, Bob?" Grinner asked.

"It's not far off twelve."

"Bloody hell, how are we going to get back to town?"

"Shit, I dunner know," Tex said, "all the buses have stopped."

Pal said, "Well, let's get to Stretton first."

As we hobbled into the middle of the village, we were confronted by a police car and a bobby standing beside it, brandishing a torch, which he shone in our faces.

Further on, another police car and an ambulance were parked up.

The first policeman approached us and said, "Is there a

Shaw, Grindley or Weston in your group?"

"Yes," we chorused.

"There has been a search for you lot, where the bloody hell have you been? Your parents have been worried sick. We've had people on the Stiperstones and all over the Long Mynd looking for you, bloody irresponsible."

After we had related the story of the hut, the fire and Pecky's loss of circulation due to his wearing wellies, the policeman suggested, "Wellies are not suitable footwear for this type of weather."

"We know that now."

"So why didn't some of you come down and raise the alarm?"

"Well," Pal said, "we only had one torch between us."

"But you did do the right thing in sorting out your friend's problem."

We got home at 12:45, thanks to the ambulance and one of the patrol cars. It was lovely and warm in the police car on the drive home. On arriving at number 17, Gran and Mum were in tears on the doorstep.

After severe tellings-off, we felt some remorse but secretly we had enjoyed the adventure and we were proud of our teamwork and the way we had coped with the situation, although the rescue services and our parents didn't quite see it like that.

Tex summed it up: "It was like escaping from the Germans in Norway."

The only member of the family on my side was surprisingly my grandad. Being ex-Army, he said to me on the quiet, "You did alright, our Roddy. Teamwork and perseverance, well done. But don't do it again and don't tell your mum what I said."

At this point, I did feel a swelling of pride, although it was ill deserved.

Luck was with us.

Playing with fire

Mr and Mrs Singh, their two sons Joey and John and daughter Jean moved into Whitehall Terrace, opposite our house. Joey, although younger than us, soon became friendly with our lot. Some of the lads asked where they had come from.

"India," someone suggested.

"I dunno where they came from, I think his Dad is an Indian Prince," I said, trying to impress.

Bob, ever the sensible realist, said, "He isn't, he flogs stockings and stuff door to door, I've seen him."

Soon after, Mr Singh went absent, leaving Mrs Singh and her sons and daughter to their own devices.

Joey spent much of his time with us and so became an associate member of our gang, being three years our junior.

On a blazing hot day, mid-summer-holiday, I arranged to meet Joey at the usual assembly point under the conker tree and told him to bring any equipment or tinned food he could lay his hands on.

I sat under the canopy of the huge tree with my head on the tent Grinner had supplied. My excitement was at bursting point; I was keen to get going and set up our camp. It was a perfect day for camping; it was already hot and the sky was practically cloudless, with just one white, lone wisp. Joey and I had agreed to form an advance party as the others couldn't come until later in the day.

So there I sat waiting, with a huge amount of equipment.

There were two tents: Grinner's, which was a US army type, made of very heavy material, and Mossy's, which was lighter, though larger. To kill time, I carved patterns on my willow staff by removing rings of bark, at the same time glancing downstream to see if Joey was coming.

I heard the corrugated fencing at the back of the garages rattle and I saw two hands gripping the sharp, wavy edge as Joey struggled to get a foothold. His head appeared with, as always, a big grin spread across his face. He hauled himself up on his arms and swung his body over, dropping expertly and, by kicking against the metal sheet, avoiding the nettles which grew against the panels.

"Come on, Joey, get your skates on," I encouraged him.

He replied, "Sorry I'm late, Mr Shaw, I had to go to the shop for me mum."

I never quite understood why he addressed me in this manner. Maybe it was because I was older than him, although only by a few years. But I must admit being addressed as Mister did make me feel like an adult. I kind of liked it.

Once on the railway line, we carried the equipment a hundred yards then went back and got another load and kept repeating the operation. it was hard-going and the sweat was stinging our eyes but we persevered.

We got to the point where we left the railway line and slithered down the bank and back again for a second load each. After going through two small fields, we came to the spot where we had prearranged with the lads to set up camp. It was in a small field, no more than four acres in total, with a small stream on one side and the Rea Brook on the other. A thick copse and the Potts Line bordered the other sides.

We pitched Grinner's tent in the corner, in a sheltered

position. When it was erected, we noticed it had a big hole at one end. But the tent was big enough to allow us to sleep comfortably at the dry end.

We settled into our campsite and dug a three-foot-long rectangle in the grass, then lifted out the turf so we could build a fire. Joey disappeared into the thicket on the edge of the field. I could hear cracking and snapping and I could see the trees moving as he searched for firewood. He eventually accumulated a large pile.

"That'll do, Joe, we're only here for a couple of nights," I said.

Pecky, Tex and Rex turned up late afternoon, followed by Mossy and Grinner, who came with their bikes. Grinner's brother Trevor also came along. Trevor was older than the rest of us and revelled in lording it over us.

Mossy said, "Give us a hand to put my tent up."

Trevor ignored him but the rest of us pitched in – literally.

That first night, we got a good fire going, having stripped the turf and dug a shallow trench. Spuds were placed in the ash in the bottom of the fire. Bean tins had their lids removed and were stood up on the edge of the main fire. After feasting on spuds and beans, we toasted bread and told made-up ghost stories.

Sparks shimmered up into the inky darkness and an owl sang hauntingly. Joey, on his first camping trip, said, "What's that?"

We chorused, "It's only an owl."

There were other night noises and rustlings which we couldn't identify. The last vestiges of light vanished behind the tall, dark trees and total darkness descended so that the only light was from our fire and the distant stars.

That first night was uncomfortable as the temperature dropped and we only had blankets fastened with blanket pins and slept on the hard ground. I had a small rock under me, which compounded the discomfort. We slept with our heads on rolled-up jumpers at the door end of the tent, and our feet under the hole in Grinner's tent so that if it did rain only our feet would get wet.

Rex settled down near our feet and I drew comfort from the dog's warmth and the sound of his steady breathing.

At 4am, the light started to grow and the weak sky highlighted the mist rising off the brook. The grass and the tent were soaked in summer dew.

I unzipped the door and crawled out on hands and knees, stood up and put on my crumpled jumper. The rest of the lads started to emerge like over-wintered hedgehogs, rubbing their eyes, combing tousled hair with their fingers, and struggling into wrinkled jumpers that had been used as pillows.

We waved tin plates at the embers of the fire, put some dried grass on the grey ash, and small kindling on top. The plate-waving and blowing soon had the twigs bursting into life. We built up the fire with bigger and bigger pieces of wood until it roared, then we stood in a silent circle around it, occasionally coughing and rubbing our eyes from the smoke.

Grinner said, "I inner having beans again and dunner give any to Tex, he was farting all night, nearly gassed the dog."

Pecky suggested, "Let's have a coffee while we think about it. Anyway, we anner got any beans left."

"Good!" Grinner said.

I produced a tin of sausages and enthused, "Look, here, we can have these with some fried bread."

After breakfast, we sat back in the tent, cradling our mugs of coffee, our heads pressed against the canvas.

Trevor shouted, "I'm pissing off now." As a parting shot, he looked at the three bulges in the canvas visible from the outside. Arming himself with a thick stick, he banged each lump with it and ran off across the field, laughing and pushing his bike before him.

He went through the thicket edging the railway line and up onto the track. The last we saw of him was his silhouette riding his bike on the side of the track.

We came out of the tent, nursing our heads, saying, "Your brother's a bloody nutter."

"You don't have to tell me," Grinner replied, "you try living with him."

"Eh, let's set the night lines," I suggested. I had four of them, comprising a wooden stake, deep sea line, a ring of lead pipe, a matchstick, and a hook. We set them five yards apart, baited the hooks with lob worms, using a rock to hammer the stakes into the bank.

We then covered the lines so they couldn't be seen but Rex insisted on jumping into the brook where we had set them.

Pecky shouted, "Get that bloody dog out, he'll frighten the fish off."

Tex whistled and ran away from the bank. Rex was soon out of the water, standing on spindly legs, shaking and sending water flying everywhere, before giving chase after Tex.

Mossy had brought a bottle of meths with him in case we couldn't get the fire going. He said, "It's funny meths doesn't burn until the last little bit. Just before it goes out."

"Give over," Grinner said.

Mossy did a demo. He poured some meths down his arm, saying, "Watch this!"

He put a match to it and set it alight. His arm was on fire.

He let it burn for a while then smothered the flame with a towel.

"Bloody hell, amazing, bloody brill!" we all enthused.

Back at the camp, we closed our tents and went under a tunnel to the other side of the track then downstream to a big pool. We called it Sandy Hollow, because of a deep sandy bank which was peppered with holes as it was home to a colony of sand martins. It was one of our favourite spots: a natural swimming pool with a shingle beach on the opposite side below the sandy wall.

The day was at its hottest as we emerged into the sunlight from the tunnel under the railway bridge. We stripped to our trunks and left our pumps on to protect our feet. From the field, we ran across the grass and made huge, exaggerated jumps, ending in screaming splashes.

After several jumps off the high sandy bank, Pecky said, "It'd be great to ride a bike off the bank."

"Great idea but who's going to supply the bike? And who's daft enough to do it?"

It was a unanimous decision it was to be Mossy's bike and he didn't seem worried about this; he considered it an honour. "I'll nip back and get it," he said.

He ran back to the camp and returned, pushing his bike, sweating profusely, and smiling triumphantly.

He posed the question, "Shall I go first?"

We all agreed that as it was his bike he had every right. He carried it across the ford at the bottom of the pool. Once up on the field, he pushed the bike about twenty yards from the bank. We all stood on the beach, shouting encouragement. Pecky told Mossy he had to get enough speed to clear the bank if he was to make it to the water.

Mossy was like a test pilot and he took it seriously. He pedalled and built up enough speed for the take-off, before heroically launching himself and his trusty steed into space, shouting "Geronimo!" as he went. The splash was spectacular. Mossy went one way and the bike the other. He disappeared below the surface but soon bobbed up, with his hand through the spokes of his front wheel. We all agreed it was a magnificent effort.

After each person had made safe landings in the brook, we persuaded Joey to have a go. He made a gallant effort, coming across the grass at high speed, but fell off at the edge of the bank and the only thing that hit the water was Mossy's bike, which slid apologetically down the sandy bank and slithered in.

"Come over here, Joe, and get the bike out," Pecky suggested.

After crossing the ford, Joey waded into the deeper water and retrieved Mossy's bike. He wheeled it, dripping, across the shingle beach and up onto the grass.

Pecky came up with the idea of pouring meths on his body, lighting it, and then riding off the bank and dousing the flame when he hit the water.

Bob said, "You're bloody mad, what if you fall off your bike?"

"Well," said someone, "we can stand by with a wet towel."

"And anyway, I inner going to fall off," Pecky asserted.

So Pecky stood astride the bike, ready for launching. He poured some meths on his naked shoulders and upper arms.

Mossy said, "Are you ready?" as he set fire to the meths.

Pecky took off like a flaming arrow, bumping across the grass, and shot into space, hitting the water and dousing the flame. Mission accomplished!

We were all well impressed with Pecky's bravery but all of us declined the offer to try it ourselves. Well, all of us but one. You've guessed it. Yes, it was Mossy.

After Mossy's leap, no one else fancied a go, so we all went for a swim, diving off the high bank. The sun was very hot so afterwards we lay in the grass above the shingle beach, without a towel between us, letting the hot sun dry us instead. Rex lay alongside us and, after all the activity, went to sleep. He kicked his back legs and emitted muffled barks as if chasing rabbits or whatever else dogs dream of chasing, or maybe he was diving for house bricks.

I drifted off and when I awoke I watched a bumble bee buzzing around the sweet clover and I enjoyed the smell of the grass.

The silence was broken by the sounds of girls laughing and screaming. 'Why do girls shriek so much?' I pondered.

Four girls arrived at the top of the bank. We all put our shirts on, bar Pecky, who was always happy to display his muscular torso to the opposite sex.

The rest of us beat a hasty retreat, with apologetic stoops covered by towels.

At that particular age, girls were taboo; it was regarded as sissy even to talk to them. I took some stick from the lads at school, who teased, "We saw Shaw kissing Daisy Lewis behind the Abbey Church."

I responded, "Shurrup, it wunner me, you made that up," as I blushed with guilt.

As we went back to camp, our sunburnt backs were on fire. We collected wood and kindling as we went back through the tunnel and into the copse. A bit more plate-waving blew the fire back into life and soon we were ready to cook. We unwrapped the chicken Mossy had brought.

Bob posed the question, "Do you think it's okay to eat?"

We all sniffed it and I said, "I think it's ok."

"Well, you've got the biggest nose, Rod, so you should know," Pecky said.

"Cheeky twat," I replied.

Everyone forgot their concerns when they smelt the chicken sizzling away in the lard.

"Chuck us a slice of bread, Moss," Grinner said, "I wanna make a sandwich."

Mossy skimmed the slice across the fire into the ash. On the other side, Grinner grabbed it, patted it, and blew it to get rid of the ash.

When we had all eaten the chicken, we wiped our greasy faces. Tex broke some bread into lumps and dropped in the frying pan.

Bob asked, "What's that for?"

"It's for the dog."

"All that bread inner that good for him, you'll make him fat," Pecky said.

"Well, who wants to give him their chicken?" was Tex's response, "And any road, he'll never get fat – look at the state of him, he's like a hairy miniature whippet."

With this, he placed the frying pan in front of Rex, who gorged himself on the bread and continued licking the pan for an age, even when it was obviously empty.

The lads sat around the fire, building it up with more wood.

"I'd better get those night lines in tonight," I said. "It's choir tomorrow so we'll have to hit the road in the morning early and we wunner have time."

We all picked our way across to the brook, using the light from the fire, as darkness thickened. When we got to the brook's edge, I slithered down to the first line and pulled it up. "Nowt there," I said.

Grinner had located the next line and dragged it in. "No bites here, either," he shouted.

I pulled the stake out of the bank, pulled the line in and wrapped it around the stake for future use. On the last line I pulled, there was a nice-sized eel squirming on the end.

Joey said, "You've caught a snake, Mr Shaw."

"No it inner, it's a bloody fish, it's an eel."

"Well, it looks like a snake to me."

Bob asked, "What are we going to do with it?"

"Eat it, you prat."

Back at the camp, I wrapped up my night lines and put them away. I skinned the eel and cut it into mini portions. Tex produced the frying pan and we all agreed we didn't want to eat anything cooked in that after the dog had licked it. Tex said, "He's got a cleaner tongue than any of you buggers. Look at it."

Sure enough, the dog's tongue looked like a piece of Spam; pink and spotless.

We settled for putting water in the frying pan and bringing it to the boil then, chucking the water on the grass, we dried it with a filthy tea cloth that looked like it had been used to clean several railway engines. We added lard to the dry pan and put the eel to cook in the hot fat.

Joey said, "I inner eating snake."

The white meat of the eel was eaten by the rest of us and generally enjoyed. By now, the night was inky-black. The fire lit our faces and sent sparks up into the night sky, to mingle with the stars. We told more ghost stories and frightened ourselves half to death before crawling back into our tents and settling down to sleep.

After five hours' broken sleep, light broke through the hole in the tent, spurring us into life. We laid Grinner's US Army tent flat and two of us rolled it up as tight as we could get it. Then we tied it to the crossbar of his bike. We rolled our blankets up and we were ready for off.

Grinner said, "Has any bugger got a comb? I anner combed my hair since I got here."

"Dunner worry, you look lovely," Tex observed.

Grinner replied, "I'll smack you up the fizzog if you dunner watch yourself."

"You and whose army?" was Tex's reply, adding, "You couldna knock the skin off a rice pudding."

Looking up to the sky revealed an ominous Prussian-blue/black cloud covering the struggling, sad sun, which was fighting a losing battle as it did its best to break through the mist rising from the brook.

"Good job we're going," Grinner commented, "it's going to piss down."

With mugs and pans, we staggered down the Potts Line with all our clanking chattels.

We parted company in the long shadow of the Abbey Church.

Another adventure behind us.

Pecky's long trousers

Dave Peck looked in the mirror on a Monday morning and saw he had developed bum-fluff on his chin. Over a period, this was followed by his voice cracking, until it finally broke.

At choir practice, he told the choirmaster Mr Stannier that he had a rough voice. Mr Stannier said, "It's simple, your voice has broken you'll have to join the men's section."

This elevated Pecky into virtual manhood, and me in the choir to senior boy soprano. It was the 'boy' bit I resented, as we had reached that age where girls stopped being pests and became major attractions.

Pecky and I were infatuated with the same girl. She lived up the Potts Line, at the back of the railway shunting sheds and workshops. She was called Jilly and had long dark hair, a winning smile, and eyes that flashed deliciously. I think she enjoyed the attention we both gave her, but that was as far as it went. We trailed around after her like a couple of love-sick puppy dogs on heat.

We had agreed to go and see Jilly on a Saturday morning. I walked down to Pecky's house to call for him. He came to the door and he was wearing long trousers. With his deeper voice, it made him appear more like a man than boy. The bum-fluff also added to his manly charms.

"Where did you get the long trousers?" I said, trying to sound interested whilst hiding the envy in my voice.

"I borrowed them off Mike, although he hasn't a clue I'm wearing 'em."

Mike was Dave's brother, who was the same size as Dave, although two years older.

We walked up the Potts Line, cut off through a gap in the wooden fence, and crossed the road to the terraced houses where Jilly lived. We didn't find her but we did bump into her friend Patsy.

"You two looking for Jilly?" she enquired.

"Not particularly," Pecky said.

"Well, she's up the footy field, top of the lane by the laundry, I've just been talking to her," Patsy replied. "Do you want me to come with you?"

"No ta," I said to the girl, who had a surfeit of puppy fat, a blotchy red complexion, and a shiny pink patch over her left eye.

On arriving at the field, sure enough Jilly was sat on a bench, watching some younger kids playing football.

Pecky greeted her first. "Morning, Jilly."

She looked up at the two of us and, dropping her eyes in a shy sort of way, said, "I like your trousers, Dave."

I foolishly leapt straight in, saying, "They're not his trousers, they're his brother's."

Jilly wasn't impressed with my response. I added, "It's a bit hot for long trousers anyway, so I left mine at home."

Pecky knew the truth and retaliated, saying, "You anner got any long trousers."

So Pecky's brother's trousers had done the trick and he sat on the bench and chatted to Jilly. I don't know what he was saying to her but she was smiling and laughing. I never knew what to say to girls, they always seemed more mature than me.

But Pecky had a sister so he knew how to talk to girls. I

had a cousin Patricia but she was only a baby and I only spoke baby talk to her.

For some time, I sulkily walked around and around with sullen, downcast eyes, kicking at mounds of mown grass and trying to look disinterested.

Like a defeated rutting stag, I turned tail and wandered off towards home, beaten by a pair of trousers.

'Jilly inner that good looking anyway,' I thought.

Back down the lane, Patsy appeared, walking towards me and looking like an overweight pirate. Her mother hadn't helped, dressing her in a horizontally striped top.

She said, "I thought you were going to see Jilly."

"No!" I said. "It's my mate who's sweet on her, I dunner fancy her a bit."

That evening at home, I asked my mother if I could have some long trousers.

"What's brought this on?" she asked.

"Well, some of the other lads have got them, even Dave Peck has a pair, and I feel left out, like I'm just a kid."

"Well, you are just a kid," she replied.

The next romantic quest we made in the direction of Jilly was a real eye-opener; me in shorts and Pecky in his brother's long trousers once more.

On arrival at the footy field, we saw her sitting on the bench with a tall, good-looking lad from the Priory grammar school. He was two years our senior, better looking than both of us, and he wore long trousers – I bet they weren't his brother's, either.

So we were shunted into the background by a railwayman's daughter, our romantic ambitions shattered. We both agreed girls weren't worth bothering with.

I moaned, "Girls always mess up cowboy and war films."

"Yes," Pecky said. "Ever notice that whenever a girl comes on the scene the cowboys go all soppy?"

I agreed, "They all go mushy and the music goes all sentimental."

"Yes, and they always try to stop gunfights, and what's the point of films, if there inner any shooting?"

"But I like Jane with Tarzan, she dunner make him into a big Jessie," I said.

"That's right, he still wrestles crocs an' all and she's a good swimmer as well."

"And she dunner mind swinging through the trees on creepers. Bet Jilly couldn't do that."

Three years later, things changed for the better. Tex, Grinner, Pecky, Pete, Bob, Pal and I stood outside 5 Belmont in Shrewsbury, looking at the sign: 'Wyle Cop Youth Club'. We rang the bell and waited. The door opened and there stood an older teenager. "Come in. What can we do for you?"

"We want to join the club, what do we do?"

"Go into the office and I'll get the club leader."

Angus McGill appeared. "So, you want to join us, eh? Good."

He left us alone in the room after asking us to fill in some forms, which he spread out on a desk. After half an hour, he returned, checked our entry forms and then welcomed us as new club members.

The boy who had answered the door came in. "I'll give you a quick tour. Please call me Gus."

He took us into the first room on the left, saying, "This is a recreation room, the girls chose the décor. It's used for all sorts of meetings and activities."

There were three girls doing summat with materials. They all looked up.

The next room on the left housed a table tennis table: "You have to book it in half-hour blocks," Gus told us. "We also have a football team and a cricket team. There is a drama group and lots of camping and hiking."

Pecky said, "That's bloody good, we're good at camping."

Through the double doors into the hall, Gus explained, "We have boxing training every Thursday and on other nights gymnastics, discos, drama, and lots of activities."

Pete enthused, "I've always fancied a bit of acting."

Tex responded, "Well you're always acting the prat, so you've got anner you."

The next room was the canteen, which was full of people, mostly girls. A pretty girl behind the counter greeted me. "How are you? I haven't seen you in an age."

I was nonplussed. She acted like she knew me. I looked at her again and then it dawned me, the penny dropped it was the pirate; the plump girl with the pink eye patch; Jilly's friend, Patsy. The puppy fat had gone, replaced by a very trim figure. The plastic eye patch had also gone, revealing sparkly flashing blue eyes: two of them.

I gained some Kudos by just speaking to her, then I joined the rest of the lads with a glazed look on my face and a bottle of Vimto clasped in my hand.

Pecky said, "Who's that? She's a doll."

I responded, "Remember the pirate, Jilly's friend? You know, the blotchy, chubby one with the pink eye patch."

"No," he said, "you're kidding."

"Honest, it is."

"Wow," he responded, "she's a stunner, what's her name?"

"Patsy, I think."

For the next few years, Pecky and I and a cast of thousands were besotted by both of Patsy's eyes, as were the majority of lads in the youth club.

There was another blonde and blue-eyed beauty in the club. Her name was Gillian and she and Patsy filled our early romantic teenage dreams. Although we all tried our best to impress her, only Pecky managed to talk to her. Some of us just stood looking, hoping the girls liked the strong, silent type. If one of them as much as spoke to me, it ignited an eruption of emotions.

It was about this time Dave Hughes and John Corbett (Corbie) became part of our group Dave brought in by Pal.

Pal Weston had two sisters, which sort of proved the point that having a sister was a big advantage when it came to communicating with girls. Pal would dance with girls and chatter away as he did so. I could never think what to talk about on the rare occasion I plucked up courage to dance with a girl. This led me to seek advice from Pal.

"What do you talk about when you're dancing?"

"Well," he said, "just get a conversation going."

"But what about?"

"Just say where do you work, or where do you live, anything that comes to mind."

So, armed with my newfound information, at the next dance we went to I decided to put it to the test. I had two pints of Butlers mild ale in the Wheatsheaf Pub beforehand, for Dutch courage.

At the club, I nervously approached the girls sitting on metal chairs all around the dance floor and picked out a small, dark-haired girl who looked reasonably friendly.

"Would you like to dance?" I asked.

She gave me a half-smile then surprisingly said "Yes," and stood up.

'Stage one achieved,' I thought.

As I did my best at a quickstep, I tried to make conversation, following Pal's advice.

"Where do you work?"

"In Boots," she replied.

I resisted the temptation to say, "Why, can't you afford shoes?" I didn't think I should expose her to my sharp wit. Instead, I said, "Have you got any brothers or sisters?"

She said, "No." Then there was silence

"Where do you live?" I asked.

She responded, "Why do you keep asking me all these questions?"

"Well," I said lamely, "I don't know really, my mate said it's a way of making conversation and showing I'm just sort of interested."

"But why?"

I couldn't think of anything else to say and turned a blushing pink and just prayed for the number, which seemed to go on forever, to finish.

I walked back to the lads, who asked how I'd got on.

I said, "She's okay but not really my type, too quiet. A bit of a kid if you ask me." Although to me she was very mature and it was me that was quiet.

Throughout my teens, I had brushes and blushes with the opposite sex, none of them very successful. Another of my failures was with a posh girl, who joined the club just after we had joined. She was very well-spoken and her name was Sally.

I had two drawings in the Youth Service Arts and

Handicrafts exhibition. I plucked up courage and asked Sally if she would you like to come to the exhibition with me. To my amazement she said, "Yes, that would be nice, I enjoy art."

As we walked to the exhibition she said, "I didn't know you were an artist."

"Yes, I've always been interested in drawing."

It was all going very well as we walked around the show. She smiled and sometimes laughed at my comments. That is, until we came to a badly drawn picture of roses in a purple vase.

She said, "That's nice."

At that point my true feelings emerged and I blurted out, "It's fucking awful."

Straight away, she took exception to the F word. I spent twenty minutes apologising, saying, "I don't know where that came from. I never use words like that." She remained unconvinced as I said, "I'm so ashamed." There were many more apologies and eventually she began to believe me.

It was at this point she came to my work. A portrait of my mum and our dog. She said, "I really like that, you're very talented."

"Thanks," I said, and explained my work.

We moved onto the next drawing, of shire horses and plough. She enthused, "I like that," to which I replied, "Fucking chocolate box crap."

End of romance!

A fortnight passed until I was at a dance in Morris's ballroom with some of the lads. We spent the evening in and out of the bar. As usual, Pal was dancing with a girl and the rest of us pretended to be disinterested.

I went into the bar, which was about to close, and ordered a pint. A slim, petite girl came into the bar, followed a rough-looking bloke. They were engaged in an argument. She had dark hair and a continental look, sort of Spanish or Italian. I found her very attractive.

I watched them and suddenly he raised his voice and smacked her across the face.

I moved closer and said, "Eh mate, there's no need for that."

His response was immediate, an explosion of anger: "I'm not your fucking mate, so keep your bloody nose out."

She pulled on his sleeve to get him away from me, moving further along the bar. A little later, the bloke nowhere in sight, she came over to me. "Will you see me home please? I know it's a bit cheeky."

Of course, I agreed. "Where is he now?"

"He's gone to the toilet."

We quickly got our coats and went up the wide, oak-lined staircase towards the street. Pete was passing and saw me walking with the girl, which gave me some much-needed street cred.

It was a good mile to her house and the boyfriend followed us every step of the way, shouting out what he was going to do to me and at the same calling her a tart, coupled with disgusting profanities. I in turn told him to bugger off, which she echoed: "Yes, bugger off, Sammy."

I asked her what her name was but, based on past experience, I didn't ask where she worked, and I was about to find out where she lived. When we arrived at her house, just behind Lord Hill's column, she said, "Thanks for walking me home. Sammy can get quite nasty."

I said, "That's okay. I don't like to see girls being slapped around."

She replied, "Well thanks," and kissed me on the cheek.

Suddenly, there was an explosion of activity, when her front door flew open. The hinge-busting exit revealed a stocky Italian screaming, "You bastard, you've been polluting my daughter!"

As I was taller than him, I wondered if I turned and faced him whether he would run the other way. But he had passion on his side so I wasn't about to find out.

I didn't try to explain that I had simply walked her home and, discretion being the better valour, I turned and took to my heels, followed by this raving mad Italian. He threatened death and may well have killed me if he had caught me.

On the way back home, I ran past the boyfriend. He turned and ran with me, both of us pursued by the raging Italian bull. Bob, who was walking home in the opposite direction, saw me, and as the Italian was gaining on me and the boyfriend I didn't stop to explain.

The day didn't get any better. When I got home, my brother was getting a real dressing-down from my dad. Apparently, he'd had a date with a posh girl and had borrowed my dad's best shoes. Then Dad turned his wrath on me, looking at my feet, raving, "Those are my bloody shoes as well! Did you know I was in the final of the Bert Lecke Bowls cup at the Postal Club and I had to play the final in my wellies in bright sunshine."

"You should have told us," my brother said in defence.

"They're MY bloody shoes," Dad responded. "Get out of my sight, both of you."

What started as an evening with some potential for a romantic liaison ended in total failure and embarrassment and an aversion to Italian fathers.

I thought he may have been connected with the Mafia and perhaps I was lucky to have got away with my life. I later found out that he wasn't Italian. He was in fact from Malta, where my mother was born, as my grandad was there with the British army.

I began to doubt whether I would ever get a girlfriend but the next Valentine's Day I had three cards from different girls, none of whom revealed their name.

'I've seen you go fishing and I don't use worms for my bait' was the message in one card.

Another had a handwritten poem. I thought she must be a posh girl.

Finally, the third had written, 'I'm on your wave-length so watch out and get ready to turn up the volume.'

I waited for weeks and weeks to get on her wave-length, which failed to materialise.

'What a daft idea,' I thought. 'I'd like to meet any of them, but don't have a clue who they are.'

My brother, jealous because he didn't get any cards, smirked his explanation. "It's probably your mates taking the piss, they must feel sorry for you."

I was left none the wiser, at a time when I was desperate to get some sort of a contact with the opposite sex.

'If this goes on much longer I could and up in a monastery,' I thought.

Girls always seemed more mature than boys, and sensible, and for me that was the main reason I didn't have a girlfriend. Also, I thought that wanting a girlfriend badly enough sort of exuded desperation and this put them off. I tried the 'strong silent type' approach. That didn't work either, as I wasn't particularly strong and the silent bit was down to the fact that, as usual I didn't have a clue what to say. Later on, I found that if you had a girlfriend, more seemed to become available.

The Big Bang at 71

Pete Jones, a school friend, lived with his parents and brothers Mike and Terry and his sister Wendy at 71 Monkmoor Road. The war poet Wilfred Owen had once lived in their house ("Not while they were there," Bob chipped in).

We weren't into poetry. but we did admire Wilfred Owen for his efforts in the First World War, which ended in his tragic death a week from the end, at just twenty-five years old.

We were frequent visitors to that happy house and always were made welcome by Pete's mum Nesta and dad Eric, who was always interested in what we were up to. Grannie Ball, who also lived at 71, was a bit of a card sharp. She held court in their front room where she taught us many card games; usually, we played pontoon or poker. She was big in personality and size. She kept a watchful, understanding, kind but disciplined eye on us over her glasses. We were in awe of her and enjoyed her company. She was like one of the gang.

As Bonfire Night approached, we were all saving for the night to come. Excitement mounted as the date neared and, come the night, we were invited to 71. Mr Jones suggested we hold a bonfire in their garden and he would run it. We all contributed rubbish for the fire so that when we arrived there was a huge stack just needing a match.

There was an old dressing table under the pear tree, where we were asked to hand over our fireworks, which were placed on the dresser. Even the bangers, our Little Demons, thunder flashes, jumping Jackie jumpers and mighty atoms ended up there. Normally, we would run around the streets throwing them at each other. Personally, I preferred to do that and kept a few bangers and Jackie jumpers in my pocket for the way home. But we wouldn't upset Mr Jones, who was a kindly man.

Mr J set off the show by lighting the fire and soon flames were illuminating the blackness. Mr Jones then placed a bottle in the soft soil and a rocket in the bottle. He lit the touch paper. "Stand back!" he shouted. There was a fizz and the bottle fell over, leaving it at the perfect angle, and the rocket scattered us as we dived for cover. The rocket made a direct hit on the dresser and the result would have eclipsed the famous Shrewsbury Flower Show fireworks; the noise of multiple bangers exploding and a myriad of colours filling the garden.

Pecky shouted, "Fucking hell!"

"Mind your language, Reverend Daniels lives next door!" could be heard above the cacophony of sound and explosive colours.

When the show ended, the smouldering dresser was pushed onto the bonfire, giving fresh impetus to the crackling flames.

Mrs Jones came out with loads of spuds wrapped in foil and placed them in the hot ashes. We all stood watching in a forlorn circle, a bit sad as it was still early and all our fireworks had gone off with a bang.

The next year, we reverted to running around the streets throwing bangers at each other, huge packs dangerously held with an elastic band. Jumping Jacks were thrown at girls, producing screams and much jumping about. Maybe

Mr Jones was right to take control of November 5th. Although we had been disappointed, it was a big event in our lives and one that lived on in our childhood memories.

We spent lots of happy hours at the Jones' house as Pete didn't take part in many of our outdoor activities and camping trips. However, in the middle of a particularly hot spell in the summer hols, Pete decided he would join us on a camping trip to Pulley Common

When he turned up, he had pillows tied to his crossbar, which was frowned on by some of us as it didn't fit in with our pioneer spirit.

It was a five-mile cycle ride to the Common off the Hook-a-Gate Road; a large area of mixed woodland next to the Rea Brook, ideal for a camp. We had the tents pitched and the turf dug for a fire, right by the Rea Brook.

Two of us had 177 Milbro Air Rifles so we enjoyed target practise with empty bean tins, after we had consumed the contents. With so many trees, the dawn chorus woke the day with the volume full-on.

Pete was first up at just 4am, complaining, "Bloody birds and that brook kept me awake. I've hardly slept."

Grinner said, "Shurrup, Pete, stop bloody moaning."

Pete did sleep nearest the brook, right next to a mini rough with some big boulders and a fast, bubbly run; a great spot for trout to enjoy the oxygen-rich water.

After eating thick porridge made edible with loads of honey and evaporated milk, we decided the first job was to help improve Pete's sleeping situation.

We put our bathing trunks on and began throwing boulders downstream, into deeper water. Some were levered with fence stakes, to shunt the bigger stones into the deeper water in the pool below. Rex was barking and doing duck dives.

The end result was a smoother, quieter section of water.

"How's that, Pete?" Pecky said. "You'll have to put up with the birds, though, we canner stop 'em singing, but you can sleep furthest from the brook."

We dried out by lying on our towels, enjoying the flickering sunshine, then set off to explore the woods as they thickened on Pulley Common towards the back of Bayston Hill.

In a clearing, there stood a massive ancient oak.

"Look at that," Grinner said and we followed his gaze up to the top of the tree where, sitting still as a statue, was a large tawny owl.

"Gorgeous, isn't he?" Bob observed.

Pecky was all for climbing the tree to see if there was a nest there. The rest of us were against it. The owl looked down on us with an imperious stare and remained statue-like, as if carved from wood. Joey reckoned the owl winked at him.

Pecky set off scrambling up to the lowest branch, with Grinner giving him a bunk up. He swung himself apelike over the branch and stood up like a white primate.

At this point, the owl took off and flapped onto a tree opposite.

Pecky explored the tree, looking for a nest, swinging Tarzan-like. He shouted down, "I can see our campsite from here and there's someone down there, by our tents."

He descended from the tree and dropped with a thud into the comfort of a thick bed of dead leaves. "Let's get back down there," he shouted.

As we got to our camp, we could see through the trees it

was Mossy. He had come under his own steam and was bending over, unpacking his gear.

"This will surprise him," said Pecky and he loaded his air gun not with a pellet but with a dart; the sort they use on targets at fun fairs. From quite a distance, Pecky took aim and shot Mossy.

"Got him!" Pecky enthused.

Mossy was jumping up and down, shouting, "Bloody hell, I've been shot! It bloody hurts, who did that?"

We all crowded around him, saying, "Drop your kecks and let us put a plaster on it."

Tex said, "We'll have to dig it out like in Westerns."

Dutifully, Mossy dropped his shorts.

Bob said, "You've hit him in the gluteus maximus."

Pecky responded, "No, I shot him in the arse."

There, buried in Mossy's right buttock, was the dart. However, only the green, blue, yellow and red feathers were visible. A ring of multi-coloured bruising surrounded the hit site.

I tried pulling the dart out by the feathers, without success, and with Mossy moaning, "It bloody hurts."

Grinner suggested I use my teeth to get a grip of the feathers.

"Piss off," was my reply, "he might fart in my face… Pecky, you should do it, you bloody shot him."

The following day, big dark grey clouds rolled in from the west and thunder could be heard far off. Apparently, you can count the time between the flash and the thunder to tell how far away the storm is. Bob did some counting and we all agreed it would be wise to break camp and head for home.

We took the tents down and rolled them up as tight as we

could, so they could be put in bags. Pete tied his pillow back on his crossbar. Mossy stood up on his pedals and we all rode home, a caravan of bikes, with Rex bringing up the rear. By now, we were seeing the odd flash of lightning.

We pedalled faster, to beat the chasing storm to our homes.

Mossy, having cycled the whole way, stood up on his pedals to prevent the dart being pushed deeper. He was exhausted. His mum took him to A&E and had his feathers removed. Loyal to the gang, Mossy never revealed the name of the sniper to his mum, or how the dart ended up in his rear. The only reward he received was to find out his arse was called his gluteus maximus – and the gratitude of all of us.

"Sounds like a Roman General," commented Mossy.

"What does?" asked Grinner.

"Gluteus Maximus, you dummo," said Bob. "It's the biggest muscle in your whole body, you know."

The ins and outs of art college

At Monkmoor Secondary Modern, we were segregated from the girls' school. Even outside on the sports field, there was a no man's land, where the girls and boys were kept apart.

It was a fifteen-foot strip and may as well have been the Berlin Wall.

During that time, I carried a torch for a bubbly little blonde called Helen, although I never dated her or even spoken to her, but she had stolen my heart. Outside school hours, she was always with a gang of her mates and I was too shy to make an approach. In fact, if she was walking up the avenue towards school, I would cross the road because I always turned bright red on seeing her.

This caused great amusement to her friends, and left me defenceless against piss-taking from mine. So, although I would have loved to have been close to her, I did my best to avoid her, and the attached embarrassment.

One blowy day in late autumn, on a bright but cold lunchtime, I stood on the sports field. Most of the lads had stayed indoors so there was only a handful of boys on the field. The girls' sector looked similarly ill-populated. Although it wasn't actually raining, there was dampness in the air.

Helen was on the field, and for once she was without her entourage. I saw this as an opportunity. I ran back into school and tore a couple of pages out of an exercise book. Back on the sports field, I quickly made a paper aeroplane. I was pretty ace when it came to aeroplane construction. On it I had written, 'Can we meet outside the Tankerville Hall Sun 4pm? By the way, my name is Rod.'

With the wind behind me I shouted, "Hi," and launched my craft. I was obviously a better projectile designer than I thought. Wind-assisted, the plane was still rising as it sailed over Helen's head, did a loop-the-loop, and landed in front of a little fat, ginger-haired girl.

She picked it up, and as I was shouting "No, no!" she read my message and screamed, "Yes! Yes, see you there," as she ran indoors, jumping up and down, waving my aeroplane, squealing and giggling, disappearing into the school.

Another potential relationship ruined before it had even begun.

There was another girl who caught my eye. She was chased by shedloads of lads in the school and was a real smasher. Sally was really out of my league. However, in an attack of new-found confidence, I asked her for a date on the Wednesday. Her reply was a standard, "I'm doing my hair on Wednesday."

Unperturbed, I said, "What about Friday?"

"No," she said, "I'm organising my sock drawer on Friday."

I got the message and called a halt on my interest in her, convincing myself that she wunner that good anyway... too much make-up if you asked me...

The best thing that ever happened to me was when the art teacher Horny Sam (on account of his horn-rimmed glasses) persuaded me to apply to get into the art school.

Surprise, surprise, I was accepted. It wasn't the full art college but a two-year intermediate course, (which we shortened to the intercourse) prior to moving on to the two-year degree course.

By now, all my mates were working; mostly in apprenticeships, and all getting paid, which put me at a disadvantage. Saturday nights, I had to stay in, so I usually mixed with my arty friends as none of us had any money.

Eventually, the lack of money caused me to leave my art course and seek paid work. It wasn't long before I got my first full-time job. I was an assistant silkscreen poster printer at Wildings. My immediate boss was Mr Rumsby; a small, semi-bald man and a chain smoker, who had a permanent stoop from bending over the silkscreen. He was sometimes difficult to understand as he usually had a fag hanging from his mouth, which impeded his speech and his eyesight.

The job ended when Mr Rumsby retired through ill health and Wildings closed the department. However, they found me another position in their picture-framing department, under Mr Wilkes. He too was an old man, who looked about ready to retire. Mr Wilkes was very patient with me. He showed me respect I ill deserved. Although I showed very little aptitude as a picture-framer, Mr Wilkes did his best and, like Mr Rumsby, he was a kind man. I decided there was no future for me in silkscreen printing or picture framing so I asked if I could see Mr Wilding, the big boss, and tell him I wanted to resign. His secretary Miss Taylor made an appointment.

The next morning, I went into the main building. I climbed two flights of stairs to Mr Wilding's office. Miss Taylor sat outside. She was a strict mauve-twinset-and-pearls lady; the silver-haired guardian of Mr Wilding.

"Knock and go in," she directed me.

I did as I was ordered and entered the inner sanctum of the boss.

"Have a seat," he said, in his ultra-posh voice. "Now, what can I do for you?"

I fell silent, tongue-tied.

He prompted me, "I believe you wish to tender your resignation. That's a shame as Mr Wilkes is retiring and you would have been head of department."

"Yes," I said, "but there would only be me in the department and anyway I'm not very good at framing, especially without Mr Wilkes."

Eventually, Mr Wilding said, "Alright, give us a week's notice and you can go. Miss Taylor will sort out the details."

On the way home, I met Pete, who was working in a furniture store. "How's it going?" he asked.

"I'm a bit choked off, really," I replied. "I've just resigned from my job at Wildings and I need to get another job."

"You want to try the Sentinel Works, there are a lot of jobs going up there and they're well paid an' all."

In the past, steam wagons were produced at Sentinel (Shrewsbury) Ltd, and later a range of diesel lorries at the same site. During the Second World War, products included turret lathes and Bren Gun carriers. In the 1950s, the principal products were buses and coaches. In 1956, Rolls Royce took over the company.

Taking Pete's advice, I ended up outside the personnel office at the Sentinel Works for an interview.

When I was shown into the office, I sat down on a chair facing my interviewer. After some time talking about my past, my family and my hobbies, he said, "Which branch of engineering are you particularly interested in?"

I didn't know anything about engineering, so I said, "Er well, er let's see, I just er, I thought maybe yes, just general engineering." I thought that a pretty good answer.

Trouble is, he didn't, and said, "Do you know anything about engineering?"

I admitted I didn't. His reaction was to say, "So what are your real interests?"

When I told him it was art, he said, "So art is where you should go."

"Yes," was my instant response.

"Yes," he repeated.

He then suggested he rang the headmaster at the art school to see if he would take me back. On the phone, he said, "I've got an ex-student of yours with me and he's interested in returning to his studies." Luckily, he didn't give my name or I think it may have been curtains.

Half an hour later, I was on the top floor of the Wakeman School, nervously walking towards headmaster Ben Hurst's office.

I knocked on the door and he spoke out, "Come in."

I opened the door and he looked up and gave me a hard look, saying with exasperation, "Oh dear, not you."

I was told to come back on the Thursday as there was a staff meeting planned for Wednesday and he would make a decision after that. On the Thursday, I was back in the art school, knocking on headmaster Ben Hurst's door. With a stern look on his face said, "Come in, Shaw, take a seat."

When I was seated, after a reminder of my behaviour before I left college, he eventually got to the point and said, "Well, after the staff meeting, they are all agreed they don't want you back."

"Oh!" I said. Stunned, I thought, 'Miserable bastards.'

He then added, "However as your work does show some

promise, I am prepared to have you back on a term's trial basis."

"Thank you very much, sir," I said gratefully.

"Well don't let me down," he added as I left the room, "See you on Monday."

So I was back where I felt I belonged, with people who listened to Stravinsky and jazz rather than pop music. Plus, there was a plethora of girls, and we were allowed to mix with them.

I didn't live up to my past reputation for being feral. Instead, I was a model of good behaviour to the point of being a toady and a swot, and although some of the tutors viewed me with trepidation, they slowly warmed to the new me.

In fact, it wasn't me who wrote in giant letters across Shrewsbury Station's bridge in Russian: 'FREE THE WORKERS OF THE WESTERN WORLD', accompanied by a chamber pot swinging on the end of a piece of string. Although I did know and admire the perpetrators, and wished I had been a part of it. Those responsible had to possess a degree of climbing ability.

Photographs were plastered over the press so I never confessed to being innocent as it added to my reputation. In fact, the inscription said, 'HOW MUCH MADAM?' or something similar. Although the local press thought it was written by Russian dissidents.

After three months, I was summoned to Headmaster Hurst's office. "Come in... Ah, Rod." That was a good sign; previously, he had addressed me as Shaw.

"Well," he said, "I've had good reports all round, your behaviour has been beyond reproach. Well done and keep it going."

"Does that mean I'm accepted, sir?"

"Yes," he replied, "you've shown a good deal of promise… all you need now is self-discipline and application and that's down to you."

"Good, thank you, sir, thank you, thank you, thank you very much."

"Okay, cut along now," he said, pointing to the door, "and keep up the good work, you should be proud of yourself."

Having passed my intermediate exam and progressed to the full degree course, I considered myself a real art student. With a grant that matched my wages at Wildings, life was looking pretty good.

Life drawing as a discipline was a must and we had an excellent life drawing tutor. On top of that, the life room overlooked Shrewsbury Town FC's ground and on match nights, every time the tutor left the room, the lads dashed for the window.

Most of the models couldn't be described as beautiful. Two were rather large and the other one skinny with weird hair.

One evening, on my way to the class, I met my good friend Ray Pearson, who was a year ahead of me and was excellent at life drawing. The life room was packed, I thought because the football club were at home.

Ray said, "Don't you know?"

"Know what?"

"Well, Johnny Parton has seen her, she's a tall willowy blonde."

"Who is?" I asked.

"The new model."

She emerged from the changing room in a dressing gown. When she dropped her gown, there was an audible gasp of appreciation. Here was a full-grown woman: beautiful breasts, long legs... in fact, she had the lot. A visual feast. Speaking personally, she improved my life drawing no end.

We recognised Jim Lucas's talent as a life drawing teacher and we had a saying: "If you want to improve your drawing, get LucasAid."

During one session, Pat the model fainted, slowly crumpling till she ended up on the floor. The tutor Jim Lucas was nonplussed as the model lay prostrate, naked. He wanted to help but everywhere he contemplated putting his hands to help her meant touching an intimate area. He was on fire with embarrassment, exclaiming, "Oh dear, oh dear."

Two of us offered to give him a hand. "Get back, get back!" he shouted. He then went and came back with a female member of staff but when he returned, Pat was sitting on a chair in her dressing gown. Johnny Parton, being a gent, had draped her dressing gown over her, covering her embarrassment.

They say school days are the happiest days, etc. Well, art school certainly fulfilled that description. I had rock climbing friends, and played football for the tech; some weekends, I played three games: the Wakeman played on Saturday morning, I played in West Shropshire league in the afternoon and for the gas board in the Sunday league. There were loads of discos and of course the annual event, the Arts Ball, which always featured big bands like Ted Heath, Johnny Dankworth and the like.

We always had invites from Wolverhampton, Hereford and Birmingham Colleges, and naturally we reciprocated. The balls had themes like Bacchanalia and Montmarte. I remember waking up at 4am in the long grass, dressed as a pixie, with bells on my hat and footwear. I was talking to the person in the grave next to me.

The town was waking up and I had a half-mile to walk home. Astonished railwaymen, postmen and milkmen stared in disbelief at this pixie in green tights, holding his head and staggering through the town. As I crossed the English Bridge a swan was walking toward me we both looked at each other in disbelieve and passed each other, Me toward home and the swan down the steps to the River Severn.

I struggled into the house and my mother said, "Bloody hell, what a state! I thought you were in bed. Where did you get to?"

"Well, er, I stayed at Alan's studio."

"And you've walked home looking like that?"

"It was the only way," was my defence.

"Get yourself a bath."

Upstairs, my brother was coming out of the bathroom. He looked at me and said, "Bloody hell, our kid, what happened? Close your eyes or you'll bleed to death, they look like a road map of Shropshire."

"Shut your face," I mumbled as I slammed the bathroom door. My head was throbbing as I had a ginormous hangover. I lay on my bed and adjusted the pillow, which felt like it was made of concrete, and spent the day groaning and moaning. Swearing I would form my own personal temperance society.

My mother came up to my room in the evening, asking me, "Are you hungry?"

At my request, she came back up with a hunk of dry bread, a lump of cheddar, and a bottle of Guinness.

The final run in to the degree exams meant less climbing on Fridays and an all-out run in to the degree exam subjects. I still had to put the final touches to my thesis, 'The English Teapot', as I had spent a week in the V&A illustrating different types and didn't want to waste my efforts. As luck would have it, one of the pieces set for the degree exam was a tea-set. On top of that, I had to prepare mounted sheets and photographs.

The summer term ended with my year getting their degree results and two of us being short-listed for the Ceramics Dept at Royal College of Art (Ally Aston and me)

Unfortunately, we had followed the studio tradition of thrown pottery and RCA was all slip-cast industrial. We both failed on the last leg and in some ways I was pleased, as I was more interested in graphics.

Oh Carole!

The other advantage of art college was the number of girls. We enjoyed mixed classes and a variety of girls from different backgrounds. Every September, a new batch came in and we loitered on the corridors, eyeing up the talent as they arrived. My first experience of this annual parade was a real eye-opener. One girl stood out to me. Apparently, she came from a private school and was a bank manager's daughter. The first to show real interest in her was Ralph Sylvester. He was the same year as me and had a duffle coat, which was standard uniform for art students and was a smooth operator.

Ralph was a good pianist and it was rumoured he had played with Humphrey Lyttleton, so he had the edge. Being a chorister was no match, and I didn't have a duffle coat. However, a slice of luck came my way. I was fiddling in my locker and Carole spoke over my shoulder, "Excuse me, it's a bit cheeky but could you lend me a piece of cartridge paper?"

Unusually, I did have a couple of sheets. I gave her both of them, saying, "You're new, aren't you?"

"Yes," she said, "My name's Carole."

"I'm Rod."

On the notice board was a poster advertising a screening of a film by French film director Jean Cocteau, at the Music Hall.

Carole was reading it. She said, "Do you like French

Films?"

I didn't know any but replied, "Oh yes, love 'em."

"Shall we go? It's on next Thursday."

On the Thursday, I waited outside the Boathouse Pub. She came down the hill and I couldn't help thinking, 'I've struck gold here, she looks gorgeous.'

In a large back room of the Music Hall, there was a screen and rows of chairs laid out, like a small cinema. We took our seats and a chap from the film society stood up and gave us a brief appraisal of Jean Cocteau. I didn't really understand what he was talking about and I have to admit I thought Jean was a woman.

With the lights during the filming there was a lot of mumbling in French with subtitles, and lots of smoke so you could almost smell the Gitanes.

The backs of our hands touched and Carole turned hers so that we were holding hands. I hadn't seen that coming. Not much of the film registered as all my attention was concentrated on our linked hands. They say between lovers there is electricity. For me it was more like a whole power station.

I walked her home and was rewarded with magical hugs and a lingering kiss. It looked like I at last had a girlfriend.

But the downside of that evening was, as we were kissing on the dark side of a massive tree, a man relieved himself on the other side, which put a dampener on the moment.

Elephant mountain

During a mini heatwave in the summer term, four of us stood behind the pottery shed, dragging on Woodbine cigarettes whilst planning a trip to the mountains. Alan, Ray, John Aston and I were all for a return to the slopes of Snowdon.

The following Friday, Ray and I hitchhiked, while John and Alan took the train to Bangor and finished their journey on a workman's bus.

We had agreed where we would set up our camp and had marked it on our Ordnance Survey maps. Although Ray and I had hitchhiked, we were first to arrive at our prearranged campsite on the shore of Llyn Cwellyn, in the shadow of Mynydd Mawr in Snowdonia, on the road from Beddgelert to Caernarvon.

We had already got our tent pitched and a firepit dug, surrounding it with big, flat stones.

"The lads will be here soon," Ray observed.

"How do you know that? Do you have extra sensory perception or summat?"

"No, I just saw the bus go down the far side of the lake," he replied, "they could be on it."

Sure enough, shortly after, the lads appeared, picking their way across the soggy marshland that bordered one end of the lake.

"How did you buggers get here before us?" John asked.

"Do you want a coffee?" Ray suggested as he filled mugs with liquid Camp Coffee, topped up with hot water and evaporated milk, it didn't taste like coffee but it was a passable drink in its own right.

"Bloody hell, it's hot," John said as he rubbed his forehead with his neckerchief.

"The coffee?" I asked.

"No, the bloody weather," he replied. "There were a few midges around when we crossed that marshland."

During our many visits to Wales, we had built up various recipes, most of them based on tinned goods of Alan's choice. If it came in a tin, it was okay by Alan, although we did sometimes get sausages and bacon, and porridge was a favourite. We made good the camp and foraged for wood, building a sizeable stockpile. There was also washed-up driftwood, which burned really well.

That first night, John suggested, "Why don't we go for a pint to celebrate our first night? Where's the nearest pub?"

I said, "It's down the lake. The Cwellyn Arms at Rhyd Ddu."

"How far is it?" he asked, concern written across his face.

Alan piped up, "It's about four or five miles."

"Bloody hell, that's ten miles for a pint," John said.

Ray replied, "Only if you come back."

"And if we have two pints, that's only five miles a pint," said Alan.

"Why didn't we camp at the other end of the lake?" John asked.

The night was starry blue as we hit the road to Rhyd Ddu, and it looked like there was little chance of rain as we stepped out. Halfway there, we walked past the Snowdon Ranger Hostel. Its lights shone out and laughter spilled into the lakeside silence.

John suggested, "Why the hell didn't we stay there, then?"

Alan said, "For one, you have to book, and two, you have to pay."

John chuntered on as we progressed onto the second stage of our walk.

Our speed increased the nearer we got to the village, as if we could smell the distant pub. Within the hour, we rounded the corner and saw the welcoming sign. Lots of people filled the bar, from locals to climbers and farmers to ramblers. The atmosphere was masculine, loud and 90% male testosterone-rich. We entered the dark interior and picked our way to the bar.

We decided on a kitty and John was first to the bar, ordering four pints of Robinson's Bitter, an excellent beer from Stockport. After our third pint, a bloke in a suit pushed open the door and entered the bar, followed by a stunner of a girl in a pristine floral dress.

All conversation stopped and the bar fell into a pregnant silence as we took in this perfumed vision of female attraction. I was transfixed and with my eyes firmly on the girl, I attempted placing my pint on the table. However, I only succeeded in putting it half on the table and down it went, smashing on the Welsh slate flags. There was loud cheering, which compounded my embarrassment, as everyone's eyes were directed from the girl to me.

I spoke to a bloke waiting to be served at the bar. "Bloody hell!" I said apologetically "That was embarrassing."

"Think nothing of it, mate," he said. He was dressed in climbing gear and I asked if he'd been climbing.

"No, no," he said, "we've been on a training exercise, we're from the RAF mountain rescue on Anglesey. Are you lot climbing?"

"Well some of us climb but we're with one that doesn't so

we're concentrating on a bit of hill walking and generally mooching around."

"Where are you lot staying?" he asked.

"We're camped at the far end of the lake."

His mates were draining their pint pots, ready for the off.

John said, "Hadn't we'd better make tracks? I'd rather walk in the light."

We left the pub, out into the still, silent evening as the light dipped behind the mountains, and set off towards Caernarvon and our camp.

We hadn't gone but a hundred yards when a lorry pulled up and the driver shouted, "Want a lift, lads?"

We piled into the back. The short journey was an experience as we were thrown from one side of the lorry to the other. By the time we got to the lake end, we were glad to get out.

We walked round to the cab and thanked the driver. He shouted, "No problem, lads."

By now, it was starting to get dark and as we cursed and stumbled across the marshland back towards our camp, some of us fell into the ditches that criss-crossed the marsh. The wind was freshening and, as always, we dug out torches followed by extra guy ropes, which we attached to front and back of our tents.

The wind helped us restart the fire and John soon had two tins of soup bubbling away in the hot ash on the edge of the fire. With some chunks of stale bread, which we toasted on sticks, it did the job. Our second course was baked potato, which had been buried in the fire.

Ray said, "What a girl, she was gorgeous."

"What girl?" I asked.

"You know, the one in the pub."

"Alright," I said, "okay."

John added, "Yes she was a real smasher."

I replied, "If wit was shit, you'd be constipated."

We put another log on the fire and enjoyed the resulting heat.

The conversation as usual turned to food and girls, which were both in short supply. Ray said, "There'll be a fresh set of new girls joining first year art when we get back."

"Yes," Alan agreed, "there's always a rush of talent, and a few posh birds, too."

We had plenty of logs from the good bleached driftwood that washed up on our end of the lake, and so we built up the fire and sat talking late into the night, sparks flying up to join the millions of stars in the inky Welsh night.

The next morning, the wind was blowing down the lake. Ray's extra guy ropes had done the trick and the tent had weathered the high winds that had blustered through our sleep. Due to the wind, we decided to seek a bit of civilisation and take the bus into Caernarvon, if you can call that civilisation.

As we skirted the lake towards the main road, we watched a man in a rowing boat trying to fly-fish, in spite of the wind. He rowed out furiously, then he dropped the oars and picked up his rod. Three casts later, he was thrown back on the shore. The best tactic would have been not to have bothered.

As we hit the road, the bus rounded the corner and stopped. We all boarded the bus. "Caernarvon, please," we said as we paid the driver, who grunted, and we took our seats amid the locals. They all seemed to know each other and knew where each boarded or got off.

There were two ladies in the seat in front of me who were

chattering in loud voices. The one lady addressed the other, saying, "I hear your Megan is getting married."

"Yes," her companion replied, "she's marrying the butcher's lad, Trefor."

The first lady responded, "Did she have to?"

"No, oh no, no nothing like that."

"Well, there's posh now, then, isn't it?" she responded.

Then they both folded their arms propping up their breasts in a defensive position and fell silent as the bus rumbled on between dry stone walls.

I thought eavesdropping could have its rewards.

(Another gem overheard in a Porthmadog pub: two local lads were addressing a third lad; a six-foot-four youth with the physique of a runner bean.

The Welsh lads asked the lanky one, "Are you going to thanksgiving on Sunday, Taff?"

His immediate response was "Th… th… thanksgiving? I… I… s-s-s-stutter, I'm diabetic, and I live in Penrhyndeudraeth. What the fuck have I got to be thankful for?")

We rattled into Caernarvon and left the bus in the shadow of the castle. Armed with one large, empty rucksack and some string bags, we were equipped to pick cockles, as instructed by Alan, who had experience in this field.

The tide was freshly out so we decided to get straight to it, removing our boots and socks and paddling out onto the flat sand of the Menai Straits.

Alan showed us the technique; the cockles were just inches below the sand and a forefinger brought them to the surface with ease. We filled bag after bag with these little feasts. Soon, our rucksack was full and we called it a day.

Ray said, "That was brilliant, we'll cook these little buggers back at camp."

We then spent an hour or so walking around the castle, which was apparently built by Edward I of England in 1283. From there, we went to a small shop and bought a large bottle of vinegar for the cockles.

John said, "How are we doing for cash? Have we got enough for a couple of pints?"

Most of us were running low on the readies but it sounded tempting.

John then suggested, "I'll do the meal tomorrow, how would you like a meat stew?"

"Great," said Ray, "but what sort of meat?"

"Ah well, that's a bit hard to predict, that's down to the butcher. Leave it to me," John insisted.

"Ok, you do the stew, whatever it is," Al agreed.

Under Alan's direction, we walked to the butcher's. A florid, rotund, red-faced man with a smile as wide as his body greeted us, saying, "What can I do for you, boys?"

John took the initiative. "Can I have six sausages and a bag of bones? We've got three dogs and they're starving."

"We can't have that then, can we boys?" The butcher grinned as he wrapped up the bones.

Armed with six sausages and a bag of bones, we headed for the nearest pub, the Black Boy. We supped up our beer and John said, "Are we having another? Where's Al?"

"He's gone to the bog," I guessed.

We looked through into the next bar and there was Alan, chatting with a pretty little local girl. She was petite and quite attractive; a sort of miniature Bardot. Ray suggested we leave him to it and get another pint in. We both sidled up to the bar and the landlord pulled three more pints.

Back at our table, we pushed our packages further out of sight. There was a distinct smell of the seaside surrounding us when a lad came over, sat at our table, leaned over and said to us in a Welsh accent as thick as treacle, "See your friend through there?"

"Yes," we said.

"Well, that girl he is talking to is wicked." He stressed 'wicked', which just made her more interesting to the rest of us. He embroidered his warning by saying, "Her boyfriend is a nasty cup of tea if you ask me and he'll be here any time soon."

We left the Black Boy and hot-footed it to the bus station. Arriving just in time, we went to the back of the bus as the rucksack was really beginning to smell.

The day was dry with a gentle breeze as we approached our stop. We jumped off the bus, crossed the road, and went through the rusty gate, which was hanging off its hinges and tied up with blue baler twine...

Feeling the effects of the beer, we staggered across the marshy land. Ray, as always, was starving. As we approached our campsite, he scoured the shoreline of the lake and came back with an armful of wood.

Back at camp, we filled every billy can, plus a few empty bean tins, with water, and cooked the cockles on the fire. Once cooked, we put the cockles in jars of vinegar. We feasted on the morsels, all agreeing the effort had been worth it. Then we moved on to our main course of sausage butties.

The following morning, I was up at first light, around 4am. Outside, it was peaceful and quiet. The lake was flat calm, with just a few ducks breaking the mirror-like surface. There were two diving birds to my right, feeding in the shallows. I thought they were some sort of grebe, as far as I could see.

Ray was the first to stagger out of the tent, rubbing his eyes. He came to the lakeside and dipped the kettle in the water. He went back to the fire on hands and knees, blew the embers, and the fire burst into life as he shouted, "Want coffee, Rod?"

"Yes," I replied.

"Well, come and wash these mugs."

John and Alan emerged as Ray poured hot water into the coffee mugs.

We stood with hands wrapped around our warm mugs, shivering in the cold light of dawn. Ray said, "What are we going to do today?"

Alan suggested, "As this is the last full day, I thought we could stay to close to home and explore Mynydd Mawr, I've camped here before and never ever been to the top."

After breakfast, we hacked some bread and took raw onion and the last of the cheese.

We explored Mynydd Mawr and decided it didn't provide much in the way of rock climbing, although it was a beautiful mountain. It is nicknamed the Elephant Mountain, because as you approached it from the Beddgelert end, it does look like the profile of an elephant on its knees.

From behind our campsite, the climb was quite steep. We progressed up a shallow valley and out onto grassy slopes with a patchwork of bracken. Once on the top, we sat down and I took a swig of lake water. We looked to the east, across the valley to the summit of Snowdon, which was clear.

Mynydd Mawr is under a thousand feet but the views to the east and south east were awe-inspiring. The clouds skittered up the valley. We watched the Caernarvon bus winding its way towards Beddgelert.

Ray said, "Who wants a fag?"

I said, "I'm saving mine, I've only got a couple left, let's get going."

We set off downhill, dropping into the Beddgelert Forest, which bordered the lake. Sunlight dappled through the trees as we made our way towards Rhyd Ddu.

Once in the village, we went to the post office and purchased five Woodbine cigarettes and a tin of Irish Stew. Then back through the village we stepped it out along the lake toward our camp.

Ray as always with his mind on food, asked, "What have we got for supper?"

Alan said, "Irish stew, baked beans, and a tin of tomatoes. Oh yes, and half a loaf."

"You're not putting the bread in the stew, are you?" Ray queried.

"Don't be bloody daft," was Al's immediate response.

"Well, you've got everything else in there."

Alan assured him that, all together in one pot, it would be great. "Ah, I forgot my secret ingredient," he added.

"What's that?" Ray asked.

"If I told you that, it wouldn't be a secret anymore."

I knew it was a jar of curry powder, but I didn't want to spoil Al's surprise.

We walked past the Snowdon Ranger Hostel, which set John off on one of his chunters, and just then the Caernarvon bus rattled around the corner. John put his hand up, it stopped, and we all got on.

As we crossed the marshland, jumping ditches, Alan said, "Aren't those your bones, John?" He pointed to a package half-submerged in the ditch water.

I bent down and retrieved the package, peeled back the paper and sniffed the contents, saying, "They're off."

John took them off me and took a sniff, saying, "There's nothing wrong with them, they hang beef for ages."

The rest of us agreed there was no way we were going to eat them.

John countered by saying, "They have been sort of marinated."

Al said, "Yes, but you can't count stagnant bog water as a marinade."

Back at the campfire, after much sniffing, John took the biggest billycan and produced onions and two carrots. We watched as he chopped up the vegetables and chucked them into the water, followed by the bones, a palmful of salt, and an oxo cube. The recipe was complete.

We had to admit John's food did smell good, probably because we were starving. John allowed us to dip our bread into the liquid. We fried some sliced bread and used it as a sort of giant crouton. The rest of us tucked into Alan's mixed stew, with him repeating, "Good, innit?" and, "You won't get food poisoning."

The one thing I remember from that particular trip to Wales was the vision of John, with sparkling eyes, nibbling the meat from those bones with great gusto, enthusiasm, and noises of appreciation. The only thing remaining was a pile of bones stripped clean, as if vultures had been at 'em. John, with a glint in his eye, wiped his beard and said, "Bloody good."

The next morning, he was up and about looking for wood for the breakfast fire. After the last of the food, mostly fried, was eaten we struck camp and headed back to Shropshire.

Thumbs up for France

Inspired by the lyrics of *Oh, for the wings of a dove*: 'far away, far away would I roam', I decided a trip to France was called for.

Carole and I boarded the Silver City Airways flight at Manston Airport in Kent, bound for Le Touquet airport; a short, channel-hopping flight. This was my second trip to France. Previously, I had been on a youth club holiday, by an ancient bus, to Le Lavandou in the south of France.

Now I was in charge and Carole had faith in me, based on my very limited youth club experience; she thought me worldly-wise.

The noisy flight was bumpy, with lots of turbulence and sudden drops in air pockets. I looked out onto the wing, where I'm sure I could see rivets jumping up and down, and the wings seemed to be moving. As we came into French air space and approached Le Touquet, I could see the runway. The landing was a bit bumpy but we were down on French soil.

Soon, we were steaming across northern France, with smoke flying in excitement behind us and Paris ahead. We were brimming with expectation and looking forward to Paris.

On arriving at a bustling Gare du Nord, Carole, under the burden of a very large backpack, turned to me and said, "What now, darling?"

"Follow me, er, the Metro. Yes, er yes, the metro." There were armed police and soldiers armed to the teeth with machine guns. Apparently, we had arrived during the Algerian Crisis. I suggested we tried to buy an English paper, so we could see what was going on.

I studied the Metro map and looked for the furthest station south. Carole stood at my side, fully confident in me. I was less confident; in fact, I was pretty clueless.

That's it, Place d'Italie – that stuck out as being pretty far south, so we bought tickets and we were on our way. There were armed police on every station.

Carole said, "Is it always like this?"

"Like what?"

"Well, all these soldiers with guns."

"I dunner think so," I replied, "but this is Paris."

Arriving at Place d'Italie, I fully expected that we would be on the outskirts, in a semi-rural area. But when we emerged from the Metro station, we witnessed wide boulevards, bright lights, and accordion-playing from busy bars and more gun toting French coppers.

I got my compass out and determined south. "This way."

Carole said, "Where will we stay tonight?"

We came to a bus stop with one French lad waiting. Carole, with her schoolgirl French, asked him if these buses went south. As she spoke to him, I kept saying, "What's he saying?"

"Not too sure but I think he's saying he can put us up at his house."

There was rain spitting in the air, so I said, "Let's go for it."

Three stops on, he rose to get up and beckoned us to follow, which we did. After a short walk, we arrived at a large suburban house. We exchanged names. The boy's name was Jacques.

We entered a large, darkened kitchen, where Jacques'

parents, his sister and her boyfriend were seated at a scrubbed pine table with an array of wine bottles. Jacques introduced us and explained he wanted to put us up in the outhouse. There were smiles all round, nods of approval, and handshakes. Jacques took us to an outhouse across the alley from the kitchen. It had a tap and Jacques produced an air bed from the one cupboard in the room. We took off our rucksacks and placed them against the wall. Jacques and I went back to the kitchen, leaving Carole pumping up the air bed. She explained she was really tired and wanted to go straight to bed. I went back into the kitchen and was offered a large red wine.

None of them spoke English and I only had the odd word of French. However, we did communicate with smiles, grunts and sign language. The mother offered me a lump of bread and some excellent goat's cheese wrapped in vine leaves, which was delicious when washed down with more red wine. I also enjoyed several Gitane cigarettes, which mixed well with the red wine. The front of the kitchen range was open and the fire within crackled and spat cheerfully.

I eventually went to bed, having shaken hands all round, and received kisses on each cheek from the mother and daughter. It had been a great evening, but I was ready for the airbed. Carole was dead to the world when I quietly crept into the outhouse. She didn't move a muscle. She looked peaceful and vulnerable and I felt protective towards her, as she had put her faith in me as if I knew what I was doing, and honestly, I really didn't.

I slipped into the sleeping bag, embraced Carole, kissed the nape of her neck, and went out like a light.

In the morning, the dawn light from a side window woke me. I felt the effect of the red wine as I lay watching Carole wash in cold water.

"Morning, darling," she said, "what time did you come to bed?"

"Not long after you," I lied as I rolled up the sleeping bag. We packed our rucksacks and were set for the off.

Outside, the sun shone joyfully. We knocked on the kitchen door to say goodbye and register our thanks. The boyfriend answered, "*Bonjour*," and with a smile Jacques followed and via Carole managed to communicate that the boyfriend was happy to drop us on advantageous position for the road south.

We chucked our rucksacks into the boot of the boyfriend's ancient Renault. After a bouncy, short trip through backstreets, we were dropped off on a corner where we would be clearly visible. More *mercis*. Using our left hands to thumb, we waited in expectation as streams of traffic roared south.

Our enthusiasm diminished as lifts failed to materialise. After two hours, yet another Citroen pulled up and we enjoyed a short lift of around 20k from a man with a small grey moustache and bushy sideburns. The smell of garlic filled the car. I think he must have been chewing whole bulbs. Carole did her best to converse with him, without much luck. She explained that she thought he was in fact a Breton, with his own version of French. "Bit like the Welsh are to us," I observed.

He dropped us at a crossroads and waved goodbye as he drove off down a leafy lane and out of sight. We went under a railway bridge, where there was a huge hand-painted sign which read '*LIBEREZ LES PATRIOTES*' in letters three-foot deep.

Carole asked, "What's that all about?"

"I dunner know, I think it's why all those coppers are around, summat to do with trouble in Algeria."

She took a photo of me against the graffiti. We crossed the road and walked towards a small village, where several people were waiting at a bus stop.

The bus arrived and the sign told us it was bound for Fontainebleau. "That's south," I said, "Let's get on." We boarded and amid some confusion we were pushed down the bus. The driver didn't seem too keen to take payment, although some people were paying. We ended up standing at the very back. The bus rattled off down the A6 south. It was a long journey and we spent the whole time standing, although we were both filled with enthusiasm to be on the move. Arriving at Fontainebleau, we were pushed out of the back of the bus and found ourselves on the pavement, having received free travel.

Across the road, on a corner was a bar with lots of tables outside. We chose one in the shelter of a chestnut tree. A waiter was soon with us and took our order. "*Une bouteille of vin rouge, s'il vous plait*," Carole ordered. She was surprised when the waiter returned with a bottle on a tray with two glasses.

"Well done," I said.

The waiter poured the first glass and put more in Carole's glass than in mine. We sat drinking red wine and smoking Gitane cigarettes.

The sky darkened and Carole, looking concerned, said, "Where will we sleep tonight?"

"We'll find somewhere, don't worry." The bottle was empty so we struggled into our rucksack straps and with the aid of my compass we headed south and were soon in the shadow of tall black trees on a long, dark road. I switched my torch on and searched the edge of the wood until I found a clear patch. Carole held the torch as I erected our small ridge tent. We were soon in our sleeping bag and, with the effects of a hectic day and the red wine, we were fast asleep.

Daylight flickered, casting shadows on the tent just after 5am, and the dawn chorus was loud and clear. I could hear running water, tinkling outside. I unbuttoned the door to look outside, only to see a French gravedigger urinating on a gravestone. He gave me an incredulous look. I had pitched our tent in Fontainbleu cemetery. This did not sit well with Carole. I cuddled her and joked, "Well, we wouldn't have been disturbed." From that day forth, she insisted we put up our tent in daylight.

We rose from among the gravestones to a bright new morning, packed up the tent, and loaded our rucksacks. We were back on the road again, with thumbs raised. It wasn't long before a lorry stopped. What luck; he was Dutch, and spoke perfect English.

"Are you going south?" we asked.

"Yes," he replied, "I'm going as far as Chalon-sur-Saone."

We clambered up into the cab. There was bags of room on the long bench seat.

"Are you British?" he asked. "By the way, my name us Kurt, Kurt Berger, and I live in Rotterdam."

"I'm Rod and this is my girlfriend, Carole."

We settled down and made good progress south. Kurt said, "And what do you two do for a living?"

"We're both art students," we chirped.

The engine hummed and the tyres sang. I looked across at Carole, who was fast asleep. I related the cemetery experience to Kurt, who laughed quietly. I struggled to stay awake myself, but felt it rude to drift off. Some four-and-a-bit hours later, we drove into Chalon-sur-Saone. Kurt pulled up alongside the river, saying, "I'll drop you off here if that's ok."

Carole blinked and rubbed her eyes. "Where are we?"

"Here, we're here."

"Yes," she said, "but where's here?"

We thanked the Dutchman and climbed down from the cab.

"Safe journey!" he shouted, as we slammed the door.

The temperature had risen slightly. We walked a short distance, until we reached a bench which looked out across the river. We took off our rucksacks and sat down to assess our situation and plan our next move.

In front of our bench was an old man in a dusty black suit, fast asleep beside his bicycle, which he had leant against the railings. To the right of him, two old men were playing boules in the misty sunshine.

Carole suggested we spend a night in Chalon and set off again in the morning. The old boules players had finished their game and came towards us. The one man spotted the little Union Jack on my rucksack. They both stopped next to us and the bearded, taller one said, "English?"

Carole answered, "*Oui*," and I followed suit.

They both said "*Resistance*," and fired imaginary guns, making *rat-tat-tat* noises with serious smiles on their faces. They insisted on helping us on with our rucksacks, then shook our hands most warmly and departed, shouting "*Vive la Grande Bretagne*!"

"What lovely old men," Carole said.

"Yes, weren't they?" I replied "they seem to like us".

"Now we need to find something to eat, and a campsite."

We walked down a long dark street in the shadow of four-storey buildings festooned with washing hung out to dry.

One building had a beaded curtain and a small sign which simply read 'Café'. The only other clue that it was a café was the delicious smell of cooking which emanated from the open door.

Carole blurted out, "I'm bloody starving."

"You're always starving," I said.

We brushed through the beaded entrance, into the dark interior, down a long passage until we came into a large, cavernous room with simple furniture.

We consumed several bowls of potage, served from a large, beautiful tureen with a help-yourself ladle. Accompanied by the type of warm bread that only the French can achieve. Having got directions to a campsite from the café owner, we put on our rucksacks, paid, and set off for the campsite.

"That was lovely soup," Carole enthused.

"Good price as well," I agreed.

After a ten-minute walk, we entered the campsite and registered ourselves, then found a pitch not too far from the shower block.

I started to erect the tent and said to Carole, "I'll do this." She found a towel and her toiletry bag and went for her shower. When she came back, the tent was up and the sleeping bag inside. The site had huge family tents with several bedrooms and strings of lights in the fig trees. Our small ridge tent looked a bit pathetic.

I loved Carole to pieces and often wondered why she was with me. She was a real trooper, rarely complained, carried huge packs and slept soundly in a cemetery. Her private school French served us well in a variety of situations. My own French was non-existent. The school I went to was more like a punishment and I learned little; certainly not French, and the English classes wunner that good.

The next day, I was awake first light and went to the shower block. After a good soaking, I felt invigorated. Across the entrance to the site was a bakers. I entered, saying, "*Bonjour, Madame.*" Then with grunted attempts at French, pointing, and sign language, I had a bag with one baguette, two croissants and two pains au chocolat.

When I returned to the tent, I looked in and Carole was still fast asleep. I filled our tiny kettle and put it on the primus stove. Then I woke her with a kiss on the cheek. "Morning, darling."

She sat up and ran her fingers through her hair, as if to comb it. After breakfast, she went for another shower and on her return we packed up the tent and our gear. We were soon on the roadside with thumbs up.

Our next lift was with an Italian, who pulled up in a cloud of dust. The drive was memorable; I gripped the seat as he overtook on bends and accelerated into straights. Forty miles on, as we approached a small group of houses on crossroads, I said "This is where we get off."

Carole joined in from the back. "Yes, this is it. Yes."

We thanked him and wished him a safe journey.

"He thinks he's bloody Fangio," I said.

"Who's he?" Carole replied.

"He's a racing driver."

We waited until he was out of sight and started walking for a while, glad to be alive. After a short walk, we rounded a corner of the road and there was a shack selling fresh peaches. We purchased four and sat on a grassy bank. I sunk my teeth into the soft, sweet flesh, which exploded with juices that were impossible to control.

Just as I had wiped the juices from my face, an old gentleman pulled over in an ancient van. I ran to it. The old man asked, "Where are you going?"

I beckoned Carole to join me and explain. She asked, "Are you going south?"

I got in the back with the rucksacks and the man's border collie. Carole took the passenger seat.

The old man was the opposite of Fangio and drove extremely carefully but safely. He hummed an unrecognisable tune as I made friends with the collie who, like the man, was very friendly. The dog soon settled with his head in my lap as we bumped and rattled south towards the sun. The dog blinked and gradually closed his eyes, the same effect came over me and I drifted in and out of slumber, enjoying the warmth of the dog.

I woke to the sounds of a city as Carole turned in her seat and said, "Rod, we're in Lyon."

The old man pulled over and we got out onto the pavement. He turned back into the heavy traffic and was soon gone. Around the corner was a large café. We picked out a table, took off our rucksacks, and sat down.

We were people-watching in what was a very busy part of the city. Looking across to the other side of the square, we noticed people streaming into a large building, which turned out to be the railway station.

We crossed the square at Carole's suggestion and explored the station. On the timetable, we spotted a train was leaving for Toulon in half an hour and decided to buy tickets as we wanted to maximise time in the sunny south.

The further south we steamed, the sun seemed to get brighter, and more and more red-roofed houses sat in the

Van Gogh landscape.

We both slept on the train, until clicking points woke us and told us we were entering the port of Toulon. There were French sailors all over the city and with the aid of our map we sorted out the coast road that would take us to our final destination, Le Lavandou. We decided on a coffee before we set off. In a bar, we met an English couple from London, who happened to be going to the same resort. They sat at the next table and picked up on our English accents.

We started chatting. "Where do you come from?" I asked.

"I'm Jason and this is Cathy. We're both from Catford."

I replied, "Well we're from Shropshire. I'm about to start work in London and Carole's on her last year at art college."

"Do you want a lift? We're going to Le Lavandou in a jiff."

"Yes," I enthused. "Great!"

Their car was a Triumph. I sat in the passenger seat and Carole and Cathy sat nattering in the back.

After a short journey, they dropped us off outside a restaurant in Le Lavandou. We thanked them and walked towards the campsite, which I had seen on my previous visit. The sea was bright blue, just as I remembered, shimmering under the sparkling sun.

We paid our site fees and picked out a spot for our tent. The ground was concrete-hard, baked by the sun. There was a shower block and a laundry room.

We pitched the tent, which again looked quite pathetic against the big frame tents that surrounded us. We sat on a rug to eat, whilst the other campers all sat at civilised tables lit by romantic strings of lights in the olive trees.

We spent the first week between the campsite and the beach, gaining deep tans. On one trip to town, we sat in a café with large cups of delicious coffee and a white couple sat next to us – judging by their pale complexion, they were probably English or Bretons newly arrived.

The man leaned towards us and said, "*Scusa moi the condiments, sil vous play.*"

"Do you want the salt and pepper?" I asked.

"Bloody hell," he said, "you're English. I thought you was a couple of Froggies."

Just then, the Catford pair bowled in. Jason and Cathy joined us for coffee. They came to tell us they were going back to London on the Sunday.

"Thought we'd find you little buggers here," Cathy said. We suggested a farewell drink on the Friday.

"Great," they said, "we'll meet you here at 7:30pm."

On our way back to the campsite, the wind was freshening and by the time we got back to the site it had grown ever stronger. Our little tent was ballooning and looked like it may take off at any moment. I always carried extra guy ropes in my rucksack, so looped them over the poles back and front.

That night, the wind was doing its best to uncover us and ruffle our confidence. At dawn, as we emerged from our tent, the wind had dropped. Outside, we noticed we were one of the few tents left standing. Some were ripped, some were flattened, and some were stuck in the trees. When the rain came, it was heavy, and as the ground was like sun-baked concrete, the water simply flowed across the surface, soaking everything in its path. Carole walked to the shops, while I tried to dry out our gear.

On the site there was a large washing area under a bamboo roof and inside were several sinks and washing lines. I had taken our tent down and did my best to hang it over a line. Also, our sleeping bag was soaked, and whilst I was throwing that over the line a French lady approached me, shouting and wildly gesticulating.

I wasn't sure what it was all about. I thought maybe I was in an area reserved for women and wasn't supposed to be there. She beckoned me to follow her, which I did. She strode purposely out of the campsite and twenty yards down the road she turned into a field where stood a large white-walled house. She climbed an outside set of steps and unlocked a bright blue door.

At this point, I saw Carole walking back from the town with our shopping.

I shouted, "Carole, come here!" The woman then showed me a dining/kitchen area and entered the small bedroom, where she patted the bed and smiled.

Carole came in the room, saying, "What's going on?"

"I think she was trying to get me in bed," I responded.

After a few *oui, ouis* and more arm waving, Carole said, "You prat, she's offering us accommodation."

When asked *combien, Madame*, she exclaimed in English, "It's free, free." She explained her name was Claudette. She had black shiny hair that tumbled down in big soft curls and a smile that truly sparkled.

After profuse thanks, we went back to the campsite, packed rucksacks, and moved to our new accommodation. I went back and retrieved our wet tent and the sleeping bag. I put them with other gear on the line at the bottom of the outside staircase.

Carole suggested we invite the Catford couple for dinner. "Yes," I agreed, "bloody good idea." She found a gingham tablecloth with a hole in the middle, three matching glasses, and a larger odd one. "Great," she exclaimed, "there are four bamboo place mats as well."

So, as previously, arranged we met Jason and Cathy and

over drinks we invited them to dinner. Jason said, "We're not sitting on a rug, are we?"

"No, we have a surprise for you," Carole said.

We left the bar and walked the short distance to the campsite, passing it by and entering the field where the house stood.

We climbed the outside steps and unlocked the door.

"What's this?" Jason exclaimed.

"It's our pad for a while," I said.

"How long's a while?"

Carole had laid the table. She had hidden the hole in the tablecloth with a jam jar full of wildflowers.

For starters, we had bought some pâté; for the main course, we had chicken thighs cooked in white wine with white grapes, button mushrooms and vegetables. We finished off with a fruit flan, which we had purchased in the local patisserie.

It was nice sitting at a table rather than eating off the floor with a plate between your legs.

After the meal, the four of us sat on the steps as the sun sizzled, slowly dipping down into the cool blue hills, the crickets at full throttle. It was truly magical. We drew on our Gitanes and finished our wine.

Jason sighed, "Great meal but we'd better call it a day. We are off first thing in the morning."

We said goodnight and goodbye, shook hands, and with kisses on the cheek, French-style, we wished them *bon voyage* as they disappeared into the warm dusk.

We finished our wine and went to our bed feeling happy and well pleased with ourselves and our efforts. It had been a memorable night.

We spent our final few days of the next week mainly topping up our tans and swimming in the sea. Anchored about a hundred yards off the beach was a diving platform with several boards at different heights. On quiet days, we would both swim to the gleaming white platform and lie in the sun between dives.

I would lie alongside Carole in her bikini. She had a beautiful tan. I would gaze at her and wonder how I had got so lucky.

On the Monday, we caught a bus into Cannes and another inland to Grasse, a town famous for its perfumes; Carole's idea.

I have to say, it was well worth it. We left the bus and wandered around the town. Perched in the mountains, mimosa spilled over the walls and perfume pervaded the air. Carole was in her element. We visited the many dark, cool interiors of a number of perfumeries and Carole sprayed lots of samples on her wrists and a few on mine.

I would have liked to have treated her to some perfume, but funds were getting low and we still had a week to go. She was happy with all the free samples and she did smell gorgeous.

On the way back to Le Lavandou, I suggested we start making tracks back to England and we agreed we would leave on the Wednesday morning. We had to allow ourselves three days to get home and that was a tad optimistic.

On our last evening we went down the steps, through the orchard to Claudette's front door, pulled the large wrought iron handle to set the bell ringing.

She came from the side of the house. We explained that we were to leave in the morning.

She invited us to visit that evening and we happily agreed.

By the evening, we had started sorting our gear so we could make an early start and we were all ready for the off, although we were really sad to be leaving.

At seven, we skirted the house and rang the bell next to the large, studded door. Claudette answered and we walked through the house to a patio area where stood Claudette's husband, Marko.

Marko was Croatian and, like many of his countrymen, very tall. "Come in, take a seat," he greeted us.

There was a large stoneware dish with chicken pieces soaking in a marinade and a barbeque with the charcoals just turning grey.

He presented a cool bottle of Côtes de Provence rosé. Cradling it with pride, he poured it carefully, saying, "This is our own wine."

It was chilled and truly great.

"What do you think?" Marko asked. We both agreed the wine was remarkable. One bottle followed the first and we feasted on delicious barbecued chicken, salads and olives.

It was a perfect way to spend our last night. We thanked Claudette and Marko for being so generous and letting us have the rooms for nothing.

They suggested we stayed on, offering us paid jobs grape-picking.

For once, I behaved responsibly and next day, early morning, we were ready for the off. As instructed, we secreted the key under a loose tile at the top of the steps. We were soon on the road with thumbs up.

Our first two lifts; one in a car and the other in the back of a pick-up truck, got us as far as Avignon. We walked through the town and out into the countryside. Carole sat on a large rock, looking down the road. The night seemed to come all of a sudden so we decided to stay where we were. The air was full of bats and the crickets were adding their sounds to the deep blue, warm, starry night

Down in the shadow of the rock was a deep, grassy hollow, perfectly hidden but close to the road. We put the groundsheet down, followed by our large sleeping bag, and didn't bother erecting the tent. We were fast asleep in each other's arms in minutes, the only disturbance being the odd set of headlights. The next morning, we arose from our hollow. Carole did her best to comb her hair and make herself look presentable, saying, "I could do with a wash and I'm bloody starving."

We were back on the road with thumbs up but there was a dearth of traffic and the chance of a lift looked decidedly bleak. The sun came up slowly, warming the landscape and casting long shadows.

We entered a village which was rubbing its eyes and waking up. The smell of freshly baked bread invaded the air. There was only one premises open and that was the bakery. We entered and ordered two pains au chocolat, two ficelles, and two croissants, all just out of the ovens.

We feasted well on them, sitting on a grassy bank, and then got back on the road. Just out of the village, Carole spotted a shower block on a small campsite. She produced her toiletry bag and towel from her rucksack and sneaked in for a shower. For my part, I used the toilet, then put my head under the tap and combed my hair.

Ten minutes later, we were back on the road, with Carole looking refreshed and as gorgeous as ever. Twenty minutes later, we were in yet another Citroen, heading north with a French salesman.

When he stopped to pick us up he said, "I'm only going as far as Montelimar." He told us Montelimar was famous for the manufacture of nougat.

"That's fine for us," I replied.

When he dropped us off, I said to Carole, "Is nougat what we call nugget?"

We called in one shop and bought two little bars of the famous sweet. By now, our money was slowly running out, and we both felt keen just to get home as the holiday was over.

One more lift and we were in Lyon. From there, we took an overnight train to Paris and slept all the way. We crossed Paris on the Metro to Gar du Nor and travelled from there to Le Touquet to connect with our flight back to Manston.

The following Monday, I was heading down to London and Carole was back in Shrewsbury, to finish her course at art school.

Adjusting to the smoke

Having left Shrewsbury with my degree in ceramics and graphics safely in my pocket, I duly arrived in London. Thinking this piece of paper would automatically secure me a job, I was gobsmacked by the difference with my home town. Everyone seemed to be running, although if you missed one tube train, another would follow in minutes. 'Why the hurry?' I thought.

Once crammed into the tube train, everyone stared at the floor or the ads. Eye contact was taboo. They just pretended to be elsewhere. Even in lifts, which were crammed with travellers, they stood shoulder to shoulder and transported themselves mentally. I sometimes got the giggles at the situation.

The whole city was wrapped in a blanket of smog, which sometimes was so thick that a handkerchief around the nose and mouth was essential.

Jack Fuller, an organised ex-fellow student, had a half-decent place in Chalk Farm with another ex-student friend, Hughie Jones. Both of them had jobs in advertising. I spent one night on their floor then set about looking for a place of my own.

The next day I spent scanning the postcards in laundrettes and newsagents that advertised, 'Young model, will fill a variety of positions', amid lots of flats and bedsits to let. A good number stated: 'No Blacks, No Irish, No animals', and one said 'No Welsh'.

I spent a night in the corner of an all-night jazz club, rather than abuse Jack's hospitality. This turned out to be a bad idea. The music was great but later on I wished they would pack it in. After a sleepless night, I emerged from the club in Soho, blinking my eyes and feeling like a newly-fledged owlet. At night, the club looked quite atmospheric but in daylight decidedly seedy.

The experience was not one I wanted to repeat but it strengthened my resolve to find something fit for human habitation. I took the northern line back to the Chalk Farm area and earmarked two possible bedsits in the newsagents. They were both in Kentish Town so were near enough to Jack and H.

I knocked the door of my first target. After a long wait, I was about to leave and the door opened and there stood a huge black man who looked down at me as I asked about the bedsit. He simply said, "Sorry man, no whites."

The next one was in a large Victorian house owned by Cypriots. It looked like it could do with a coat of paint. However, on seeing the room, it was big enough and the price was right, so I took it.

The room backed on onto a railway, which rattled the putty in the windows, so sleeping was difficult. Also, there was a problem with the lock on my door. It didn't have one!

In fact, the door latch didn't engage properly, so you couldn't even shut it. At night, I propped an *Evening Standard* against the door so I would know if anyone tried opening it.

In the early hours, I heard the sound of newspaper moving, in contact with the linoleum. I woke and was very quiet, trying to memorise where the nearest light switch was located.

A train rattled past, breaking the silence. After that, the one sound I could hear was my own heavy breathing and more newspaper against lino.

I counted 3… 2… 1… and leapt up, grabbing for the light switch. When the light came on, I looked straight at the door and it was all intact, still shut with the newspaper still in place. The source of the sound was the newspaper I had dropped to the floor prior to me dropping off. My own movement was rustling the paper by my bed. I stood shaking in my boxer shorts, relieved and feeling a tad stupid, and pleased that no one had seen my panic.

The following weekend, I made a concerted effort to search for another bedsit. I left my case and set off with just a notebook, a pen, and determination. One look at Hampstead village and it was painfully obvious that it was out of my price range. I visited several potential homes and found them much the same: a baby Belling, a sink, a bed, and some newspaper beneath. Sometimes the paper had yellowed with age and was weeks old. The walls were devoid of paint or pictures, or any sort of charm.

After a disappointing search, I rang Jack and suggested we meet for a pint later.

"Glad you rang," Jack said, "there's a room come up at our place, it's on the floor above us."

That evening, I went to Chalk Farm and met the landlady, Mrs Winter. She seemed to set great store by Jack's endorsement of me and at last I had a pad. It was clean and tidy, although the bathroom was shared and was down a short flight of three stairs, with an archaic water heater at the tap end.

Mr and Mrs Winter lived in the basement. Mrs Winter liked to see herself as upper class, but her accent was anything but. She came out with phrases like, "We went to a concert at The Royal Halbert All," and, "My son's got a Triunth motorbike."

I took the room and at last I felt fairly settled and began picking up regular work from BBC TV, at Television Centre in Shepherd's Bush. Things were looking decidedly brighter. Jack and Hughie both had jobs in advertising. Al Rogers, one of my climbing buddies, lived close. He was a student at RCA so I kept in touch with him, and Bob, another of my childhood mates, took a room in a road around the corner, after leaving the army having completed his national service.

The winter of discontent

On a wet night in April, the three of us had enjoyed a few pints in Ken's Bar, at the bottom of Primrose Hill Road. Jack and Hughie took off home, leaving me with the dregs of a pint to finish. But the real reason I had stayed on was the beautiful Russian girl sat at the bar. Tamara Alferof had silky, straight natural blonde hair, and a smile that would make any male go weak at the knees. In my case, it made me weak all over and I had carried a torch for her over several weeks. I went back to the bar and ordered another, perching myself on a high stool with her between me and the bar. I watched as Ken pulled me a pint and placed it on the counter then said, "Excuse me," as I leaned across in front of her.

She leaned back, smiling. "That's ok."

Instead of picking up the glass carefully, I used just three fingers through the handle, in what I thought looked pretty neat. A bit James Bondy.

Mistake! The whole pint pot swivelled and I poured the beer in her lap. She spurned my offer to sponge her down, which was not surprising. So ended Anglo-Russian relations. I slunk out of the bar apologetically, stooped like a dog who had just messed on the carpet. I can only describe as feeling a total prat.

On the way home, I got taken short and called in at a public toilet. Following feline sounds, I found a small tabby cat crying out for attention. I picked it up. It was like a bag of bones and in a very distressed condition. Foolishly, maybe,

I decided to take it home and feed it. It was so thin I called it Twiggy, although I wasn't sure of its sex. When I approached my digs, I put it up under my sweater, as animals were *verboten* as were females.

Once in the room, I locked my door and let Twiggy out. I opened a tin of Spam, fried a couple of slices and chopped them into a saucer for her. She gorged on it, as if she'd never eaten before. I put an old jumper in a cardboard box for her bed and placed it on the floor, under the tele.

It didn't take long for Twiggy to recognise the comforts of my bed. I looked down as she curled up near my feet then I switched the light off with a comfortable feeling that I had acquired a mate.

Carole was a frequent visitor to London for weekends, which had meant sneaking her into my room as Mrs Winter didn't allow girls to visit in this way.

During her visits, we mostly spent our time in art galleries and jazz clubs, where jive was the dance style we both loved.

On Saturday morning, Twiggy was cuddled up between my shoulder blades. I locked Twiggy in my room and popped down to Jack and Hughie's. I told them about the night before, leaving out the bit about Miss Alferof. Instead saying, "I spent the night with Twiggy, come up and meet her."

Jack's reaction to Twiggy was, "Nice cat, but Mrs Winter doesn't allow animals."

My mates agreed Twiggy had pulling power. Hughie, being practical, said, "Where is it going for a crap?"

Jack shot out of the room and came back up the stairs with a large biscuit tin. "All we need is some soil, and we can get that from Primrose Hill."

As it turned out, it was the cat that was to prove my undoing.

They say bad things always come in threes. Or was it good things? Whatever, in my case it just happened to be bad things.

First thing one day, I woke early and the toilet beckoned. I jumped out of bed, walked along the landing, took the three steps down to the shared bathroom. There was a light on, the door shut, and steam on the glass, so I went down to the toilet on the floor below. What a relief! On my way back upstairs, I passed Mrs Winter and said, "Good Morning, Mrs Winter."

She gave me a look of total disgust. Back in my room, it suddenly dawned on me – still half asleep, I looked down in shock, I was totally starkers.

Number two came on a sunny May morning. I was in my room enjoying an after-breakfast fag. In the back yard, Mr Winter had a large piece of lino he was preparing to cut for their kitchen. I flicked my dog end out of the window. It landed on the lino and burned a small area. The perpetrator question was easy as I looked over the yard and I was the only one who smoked.

After a severe ticking off, my third misdeed followed shortly after. I asked Jack, "Have you seen the cat?"

"No," he said, "I'm going down to pay my rent, will have a scout round after." When he returned, he told me that Mrs Winters wanted to see me.

I knocked on her door and she shouted, "Come in." She guided me into their lounge, saying, "Just look at this."

There was a round, beautifully polished mahogany table. Scattered all over it was soil from a shallow bowl and lots of crocus bulbs.

"And he's done his business in it."

As I was getting an ear bashing, words came to my mind:

'the cat crept into the crocus bowl, crapped and crept out again'. I couldn't suppress a smile.

"It isn't damned funny, you know you're not allowed animals so get rid of it," Mrs Winter ordered.

"Where's Twiggy" I asked.

"Mr Winters threw it out of the back door," she said triumphantly.

Jack, Hughie and I searched for the cat with no success. Eventually, we decided on going for a pint, and as we passed the public toilet Twiggy appeared, so pleased to see me. I picked her up and went back to the house. Jack went ahead to see the coast was clear. I put her in her bed and locked the door.

That night, Twiggy went to sleep on my chest, purring and bunting me under the chin. This show of affection made me think of taking this cockney cat to enjoy a new life in Shropshire. On Friday evening, I was boarding the train from Paddington to Shrewsbury with one suitcase containing my dirty laundry and a holdall containing a tabby cat.

Once at home, my mum opened the case and took my laundry up to our wash-house.

Then she said, looking at the holdall, "What's in here?"

"Open it," I said.

When she unzipped the bag, out popped Twiggy.

Brother Tad said, "It's lovely. where did you get it?"

My mum was noncommittal, but my dad complained, "What you going to do with it?"

"Leave it here, it was starving in London and anyway the landlady said it has to go."

Gran said, "It'll be company."

Gran would have been on my side even if I'd have brought a gorilla home. So to cap it all, Twiggy had a new home and

I knew I'd done the right thing.

On Sunday night, it was back to the Smoke with my childhood mate Pete and a suitcase full of clean clothes. Pete was looking for a well-paid job to pay off some sort of a business debt. I explained to him that that I was experiencing the Winter of Discontent as Mrs Winter wanted me out.

The plan was to find two bedsits, or a big one that would accommodate the two of us. In the meantime, I told him he'd have to kip on my floor.

Monday morning, I briefed Pete to first look in the newsagents and then the laundrette.

After an unsuccessful morning looking for freelance work, I met Pete in the Queen's at lunchtime. He'd made progress but was unimpressed with the results. "There is this one on Primrose Hill, sounds ok, the landlord doesn't live there but he's promised he'll be there after two today."

We found the building at the far end of the hill and rang the bell of the Victorian house, which had four floors and a basement flat. The landlord answered the door. He had black hair plastered down with Brylcreem and a sallow, unhealthy complexion.

The room was massive, on the ground floor with a huge bay window looking out onto the hill, with a cubicle galley for cooking in one corner. There were three beds – two down one side and another across the end. "When can we move in if we wanted to?" I asked.

"Soon as you like," he replied, "the previous people did a runner without paying."

"What are the costs?" Pete asked

"Well, you have your own meter, which takes 10ps. It sleeps three comfortably and it's £250 a month, so I would get another person to split the costs three ways. Think about it, I'll be upstairs for a while."

"What do you think of it, Pete?"

"It's big enough and if we can find someone else to share, it's cheap enough."

Thanks to my trio of mishaps, I'd been given my marching orders by the Winters, with a week's notice to find a new pad, so I was keen to find somewhere and Pete said, "Yes, let's go for it."

After a tap on the door, the landlord poked his head around, saying, "Well lads, made a decision?"

"Yes! We'll move in Wednesday if that's okay."

In the meantime, we put cards in the laundrette and newsagents to share an apartment on Primrose Hill. Pete said, "Bob's moved to London after conscription, let's go and sort him out." We found him in one of the smallest bedsits; there was one chair, a single bed, a small table with double gas rings, a frying pan, and that was it.

He turned us down as he was very much the recluse and liked being alone. Back at my room, we were discussing tactics when Jack came up with Ally Aston another Art School mate.

I shook his hand "How you doing, mate? Where are you staying?"

"At the moment on Jack's floor," was his swift response.

"That's brill," was Pete's reaction to Ally saying he'd be happy to make up the trio, actually proving good things also come in threes. Split three ways, the rent would drop from £125 each month to a rounded-up figure of around £85, so it was good news all round.

Moving day was quite a simple affair. The key had been left in the door and after four or five suitcases were chucked on the beds, we were home and dry.

We sat down and picked our beds; Pete first because he found the place, me next, and finally Ally, but it didn't matter as they were all much of a muchness.

Pete was sat looking out through our net curtains, saying, "There's a helluva lot of people going in and out. I'm going outside to see just how tall this place is."

"While you're up, stick the kettle on," I suggested.

After a cup of tea, we went food shopping and ended up in the Queen's for a couple of pints. We agreed that this would be designated as our local and so it came to pass.

We settled down in Primrose Hill. Bob was a regular visitor and Ray came over from Muswell Hill occasionally. With Hughie and Jack a stone's throw away, we established a bit of Shropshire in the Smoke.

Pete found a job in sales at John Barnes Store on Finchley Road. He also found himself a girlfriend, who also worked at the store. Kathy was a nice quiet girl from Northwood Hills. Most Sundays, Pete would go on the tube and enjoy home-cooked meals at her family home so we didn't see much of him.

Al had a decent job at a small agency in the city and my freelance work was increasing. A steady supply from BBC Television, British Rail, and bits from *Radio Times* and one or two publishers kept my head above water.

So we were well set up for the swinging sixties. Primrose Hill was the place to be and our large room a great party venue.

One weekend, the lads were off home and I ended up on my own. Saturday night, I walked up to the George

Washington pub and on towards the Belsize Tavern. I heard music blasting from a large Victorian house. It was coming from the top floor.

I popped into the Belsize Tavern, had a pint and bought a half-bottle of wine. With the bottle in my pocket, I went back to the party house. As the front door was open, I went in and climbed up three floors. I could see along the landing that there was a room on the right with bright light spilling out. Beyond that, there was darkness and a blast of sound so if I could get past the shaft of light I would be in the safety of darkness.

I strode in boldly, put my wine on the table, and poured myself a whisky. Taking a sip, I looked around the room and as my eyes adjusted to the darkness I could see I was the only white man in the room. The place was jumping when a tall black guy approached me.

I said, "I stand out a bit as a gate crasher."

His response was, "You're alright, man, it's my pad, I'm Conroy." He shook my hand and said, "Enjoy."

The jazz was good and the atmosphere was joyous. At the drinks table there stood one of the handful of white girls. She addressed me, saying, "Gatecrasher?"

"No," I lied, "Conroy invited me." Changing the subject, I asked her, "What's your name?"

"Sheba," she replied.

"Nice name."

"It's Jewish. My real name is Bathsheba. My mum's idea, it's something out of the Bible I think she married King David."

Sheba was a joy to the eye; lovely contours, intelligent light brown eyes, and a dark bob haircut which framed her face and emphasised her long neck. One of her friends shouted, "Sheba!" and she was gone into the light of the kitchen

As the party rolled on into the early hours, I was feeling a tad pissed and knew it was time to go. My head was beginning to throb and I was in need of fresh air.

As I descended the stairs, I bumped into Sheba, who was also leaving. "Would you like me to walk you home?"

Her response was a mumbled, noncommittal, "Err, ok."

I walked her to her flat in Fitzjohn's Avenue, which was in the opposite direction to Primrose Hill. At the front door, I attempted to kiss her. She turned her head, which meant I kissed her cheek. She then explained she had a boyfriend in Golders Green. I in turn told her about Carole.

"We could be friends, though," I suggested to Sheba.

"Why not? As long you understand it's on a friends-only basis," she agreed.

I said, "I'll see you around, then. Night."

On the Sunday morning, I was on my third cup of coffee, trying to foster some sort of normality. There was a knock and the landlord came in. "I won't disturb you, I've just come to empty the meter."

Shit! was my reaction. We had devised a method of controlling our energy costs. We employed a miniature landing net with a woman's hairgrip and a piece of nylon stocking secured at each of the open sides of the grip. This, with the help of sixpence piece, allowed us to work the net through a small gap between the meter and the cash box. When we had secured our energy, we would then work our landing net back through the gap.

I knew we had given it some hammer. I sat quietly, pretending to be engrossed in my book.

"I smell a rat," exploded the landlord. "Last month there was over thirty quid in your meter. Don't tell me you've only used a shilling's worth of power this month. You're a bunch of crooks."

"Sorry," I said, which seemed inadequate.

He said, "I'll estimate what I think you would have used and you'll have to cough up."

"Ok," I agreed, "the others are back tonight."

The penny had dropped for the landlord, who then sent a workman to make some security additions to the meter. It spelled the end of our landing net scam.

Coming up to my birthday, with Sheba in mind, I suggested a party and a flat-warming. Bob, ever the pessimist, said, "We dunner know any bugger."

"All you need is loud music and an open door," I assured him.

Five of us went down to the Queen's, leaving Bob in charge, convinced no one would show. We had a couple of swift pints and Alan suggested we return or Bob may be getting lonely. As we approached the house, we could hear party sounds blasting into the night air.

There were two lads at the door, acting like bouncers. The taller of the two said, "You can't come in, it's packed to the gunwales." It took some time to convince them that it was our place. Once inside, our room was packed and awash with booze.

Bob was bopping with a small girl and for once had a smile of enjoyment on his face. I looked around for Sheba but there was no sign of her, in spite of my personal invitation. There was still bags of action well past midnight and then people started drifting out. Not in a tidal wave, more as a dribble. The last of our guests left and I went to the bathroom and then back into our room.

I was surprised to see a shock of black hair strewn across my pillow. I pulled the covers back to find I had a girl in my bed. After failing to rouse her, I stripped down to my boxer shorts, pulled the covers back and pushed in next to her saying, "Cutch up, dear." She cuddled up to me and the warmth of her body was comforting against my back.

When I woke in the morning, she was still dead to the world. She was a pretty girl, although a bit worse for wear. She used my shoulder as a pillow and I touched her on the cheek, saying, "Morning." She was then half-awake and I said, "Can I introduce myself?"

Her reaction was accompanied by a puzzled look. "Why! And who the fuck are you?"

"My name is Rod and this is my bed."

"Oh, sorry, my name is Jackie." She had light blue eyes that contrasted with the blackness of her hair. She slipped out of bed, threw a dress over her head, and stepped into her shoes. "Bloody hell, I'll have to go, got any coffee?"

She polished off her coffee and said, "Nice to meet you, Rod, great party, see you again." And she was gone.

Alan said, "You did alright there, good-looking girl, are you seeing her again?"

"I dunner know – maybe or maybe not." I didn't tell him nothing had happened. I would have liked to have seen her again, but I didn't even get her phone number. I suppose that was the sixties swinging.

The lads rose from their beds and we set about tidying up the room, which looked like there had been a terrorist attack. Bit of a nightmare, but a great party and there were bonuses: three unopened bottles of wine hidden behind the curtains, a half-full bottle brandy and some cans of lager under the beds, and we soon whipped the place into shape.

The following Saturday morning, we came back from our weekly shop. It was a raw day, with a sense of snow in the air. We put the shopping away and relaxed with a glass of brandy (a present from Ally's uncle). I popped to the toilet and on my way back, the front doorbell rang. I opened the door and on the step was a black man, saying, "I've come about the room."

"Ah yes, the room. I can show it to you, come in, but the landlord doesn't live here."

The room was on the same floor as ours at the back of the house. But, unlike ours, it was ridiculously small. It was dark, oak-panelled, with a table, a single bed, and a double gas ring. One window afforded a view up the garden if you stood on the bed, and that was about it.

He liked it, so I said, "I'll ring the landlord and see if it's still available. If you go down to the pub down the road called the Queen's, we'll be down asap with news."

He left with a broad smile on his face.

I rang the landlord and told him someone was keen on the room. "Great," he said. "It is vacant and I could do with letting that one."

"So can he have it?" I added, "Oh there is one thing, he's black."

His attitude totally changed. "How black is he?" he asked.

"He's as black as you can get, he's a real black African from Ghana. He works for the Bank of China and he's dead smart."

"Well, I have to think of the other residents."

"So if I ask them if they don't mind letting him have the room can I offer it to him?"

"Well, er, I don't, you know, er I suppose so."

I started on the top floor and asked the two old ladies how they felt. "No problem," they said.

Next floor down, I had a similar result from the two Jewish girls and Ted, a Jewish lad who wasn't connected to the girls. His response: "No bother."

In the basement were two Swedish girls and a Roedean girl. One of them, Ula, said, "That was some party you had the other week."

I replied, "I know, I'm sorry."

"About the black guy, we don't mind if he moves in."

"Good. I'll make sure you'll get invites if we have another party."

I rang the landlord, telling him everyone was happy to let the room.

Pete had gone to Kathy's for Sunday lunch, so it was down to Alan to go to the Queen's and tell the man I was on my way.

I ran down the hill with the good news, walking into the Queen's, and saw Alan was sitting with the hopeful man. He looked towards me and I gave him the thumbs-up with both hands and walked to the bar. He leapt up, saying, "I'll get that."

I said, "No, you're alright."

He insisted. "So I take it I've got the room, when can I move in?"

"Now, if you want," I said. "I have the keys."

I asked him his name.

"You won't believe it," he said, and he was right. It went something like this: "It's Kofee, Kenna, Appiah, Amoah, Coo Attah. But you can call me Ken, and I go by Ken Amoah."

Ally said, "Bloody hell, that's a relief."

And so, on the Monday, Ken moved in and we had a real

African as a neighbour and potential friend, which proved to be the case. Swedish girls in the basement flat and Jewish girls on the first floor completed the picture. Ken, Alan and I spent lots of time at parties, invited and uninvited. Jazz clubs like the Flamingo and Ronnie Scott's. We saw Carmen McRae at the Flamingo Club, went to Louis Armstrong, Ella Fitzgerald, and MJQ concerts and lots of British greats. At times, Ken was a bit embarrassing. If he liked the music: he would grunt "Yeah! Yeah! Yeah!"

Pete, however, lived his life between work and Kathy and if he had stayed in London he would have turned London into Shrewsbury. On a bitterly cold Monday morning, Pete was up early, dressed and ready for work.

Alan said, "Look at him, he's going places."

"Yes," I replied. "Finchley Road."

If on the odd occasion he was with us on Sunday, we had to do a roast lunch just after two and spend the afternoon lying about reading the Sundays, just like home.

Early December, coming back from the Queen's on a Saturday, temperatures were plummeting and a million stars scattered across the clear cold night.

On the Sunday, it was as if a blanket had descended, silencing the morning.

I poked my nose over the bed clothes, got out of bed, put my slippers on, and staggered to the window, opening the curtains to see everything obscured by a massive snow fall.

I excitedly told the lads and all they did was make inaudible grunts and go back to sleep.

I went to the front door and it was a case of snow had fallen, snow on snow. I gave Ken Amoah's door a knock, saying, "Come and look at this!"

He followed in his dressing gown. When I opened the door, the look on his face was unforgettable. It was the first time he had seen snow. He said, "My God, what will they do with it all?"

By mid-day, the hill was covered with toboggans, skis, and anything else that would slide. The snow lasted for days and days. The Queen's enjoyed a bonanza of new customers, it was more like St Moritz than North London.

This was the start of the sixties and we were all set to make the most of it. Ken had settled in and we were on speaking terms with the Swedish girls and Miss Jeffreys, their English friend. Carole would finish her degree the following year and would be welcomed with open arms. As for the cat, my mum rang to say, "Twiggy is definitely a female, she's just had six kittens."

So, all around, the future looked pretty interesting.

A month in the mountains

At art school, I had soon found kindred spirits in Ray Pearson, Alan Rogers, Hughie Jones and Nic Parry. All good artists and committed rock climbers, and when it came to rock climbing, I adopted a Walter Mitty attitude.

My only previous experience amounted to a weekend of mountaineering in Snowdonia with Wyle Cop Youth Club. Nevertheless, I saw myself as a cross between Sir Edmund Hillary and Sherpa Tenzing. But I fitted in and soon found myself following Alan Rogers up the Milestone Buttress on Tryffan in North Wales. Although it was raining and the rock was slippery wet, I was hooked and from then on looked at mountains and rock faces in a different way.

Alan was in a higher division when it came to climbing, but he did pass his knowledge on to me. He always led climbs and I followed on with the safety of the rope to overcome my fear of heights.

Visits to Snowdonia became a habit and rock-climbing an obsession. Often on Friday mornings, two or three of us could be found on the A5, thumbing lifts to Snowdonia and missing lessons on a Friday.

This all became more difficult once we were settled in London.

Most Thursdays, I would meet my friends in London at the Samuel Whitbread Bar in Leicester Square, and the conversation usually turned to rock-climbing and girls. In that order. On one such Thursday, after a couple of pints, we decided a trip to North Wales was on the cards. For us, rock-climbing was not just called for; it was a necessity. We were all fed up with claustrophobic London and sweaty tube trains, and yearned for fresh air and the freedom of the mountains.

Term ended for Alan and he left the very next day to start his summer break. A week later, Ray and I took the train from Paddington to Shrewsbury and had a weekend with our families while sorting out our tents, rucksacks and climbing gear.

We bought train tickets to Caernarvon and Ray and I met at the station to catch a stopper to Crewe. On arrival at Wem, we shouted down the platform to Alan, who was walking towards us and boarded the train. We were all excited at the prospect of an extended stay in the mountains.

At Caernarvon, we caught a bus to Rhyd Ddu, where we stocked up with some extra food at the post office and set off up the track towards the summit of Snowdon. This was one of the less challenging routes and an easier option for the less experienced.

At about 1200 feet, Alan said, "We go right here," and we cut off through some marshy ground, through a boggy gateway, and squelched on. Alan said, "I've picked a camp site for us; found it last time I was here."

When we came to the site, it was pretty good. There was a ten-foot outcrop of rock, sheltering us from the north winds that blasted up the valley from the direction of Anglesey.

Ray said, "It's good, but where's the bloody water, Al?"

"Don't panic, there's plenty over here."

Twenty steps to the north-east there was a small, disused quarry, twenty feet deep and twenty feet across. At the bottom of the quarry was a lovely little pool that you could jump across. Alan had a length of old hemp climbing rope. He tied it at the top and threw it down towards the water supply. "It's potable as it comes straight out of the mountain," Alan assured us.

We pitched Alan's roomy three-man tent and a little single tent next to it, to store provisions and equipment. I took a short walk from the tents up onto a grassy ledge and sat looking towards Anglesey. Focussing my eyes over twenty to thirty miles after being in London, where you mostly only focus in yards, it was a joyful experience and imbued a sense of much-needed freedom, relief and well-being.

"Rod!" someone shouted, which carried on the wind and disturbed me, so I ran back to camp. Ray was off foraging for wood and Alan said, "Fill that water container." It was fairly large with a tap at the bottom and I used a secondary thin rope for hauling it up.

I abseiled down the fix rope to the pool, sank the container in and pushed it underwater. It glugged up the water like a thirsty dog.

I tied it off and climbed back up, using the fixed, knotted rope. Once at the top, I hauled our valuable water supply up to our campsite. It all worked well.

Alan took on the job of cook and Ray and I were his lackies. Alan's signature dish was fried Spam and tinned potatoes, or his tinned Irish stew with tins of carrots and beans.

I said to Ray after Al's first dinner, "Al's no chef."

He replied, "He's no bloody cook, either."

"Never mind, he likes doing it, so let him get on with it."

So we got used to tinned sausages, beans and eggs that were somewhere between fried and scrambled. His porridge could have been sliced, it was that thick, and Ray and I would argue about who should clean the saucepan.

As you abseiled to wash dishes in the brook, you could wipe around the pan to secure the residue and eat it off the side of your hand.

In the tent at night, especially when it was cold and raining, Alan would tease Ray, saying, "Imagine Jenny in a see-through baby doll nighty, bringing you a gammon, broad beans and chips. While you wait, sipping a glass of wine beside a roaring log fire." Jenny was a well-endowed scrumptious fellow student.

"Shurrup, Al. I'll bloody kill you, Rogers."

We would all go to sleep with Alan's description implanted in our brains.

I wasn't sure whether it was the idea of the gammon, the delicious Jenny, or the roaring fire which was torturing me.

On our first morning, after a damp night, I unzipped the tent and on hands and knees crawled out and stood up, rubbing my eyes. I urinated with the wind, looking down the valley at clouds weeping rain.

Alan emerged from the tent, mumbling, "Lovely day."

"You're bloody joking," I moaned. Well, at least it had stopped raining, I thought, but it could hardly be described as a nice day.

Ray soon emerged.

"Sleep okay, Ray?" I greeted him.

He responded with, "Yes, slept like a baby, I'm bloody starving."

"Well, get some wood in and we'll get the porridge on the go," Alan ordered.

After a sizeable portion of Al's super-thick porridge, with lashings of sugar and evaporated milk, we surrounded the ordnance survey map and planned the area we wanted to climb. Alan always led and we had a good day's climbing. Al's idea was to try and put up a new route and get it included in official guides. We ended up south of the summit in Cwm Tregalan, where we found some good routes; everything from difficult to very difficult, and some shorter pitches, which Alan classed as severe.

On the way back – Ray, as ever, starving and keen to find a meal – we discovered an old building; the remains of a wheelhouse or something to do with mine workings.

During our time on Snowdon, we did lots of climbs, confining ourselves to the mountain and staying out of the village pubs. This was all down to Alan, who wanted the Spartan life and all our energies concentrated on climbing.

When we ran out of supplies, we had to go down to Rhyd Ddu, usually in the mornings. Dressed in shorts and a cycling cape, we would run down to the village and buy our supplies. Alan timed us there and back and it became competitive. I held the record.

The second time I went, however, on arrival in the village I went straight to the café and ordered tea and a buttered scone. I drank the tea and ate some of my scone, and I finished it off as I made my way back to camp.

On another day, when it was my turn to go down for porridge, spuds, bacon and tea bags, the clouds were skittering across the wet landscape as I set off downhill. Ray said, "I'll come with you, I'm out of fags."

The two of us ran, jumped brooklets, and skidded downhill towards the village.

On arrival, Ray said "There's a café here, shall we have a cuppa?"

After wiping our feet quickly, we entered and the girl behind the counter said, "Usual, boys?" It turned out that Ray, like me, had been cheating and enjoying the forbidden fruits.

We left the café, crossed the road, and began the slog back up to our camp. Ray enthused, "I wouldn't object to a trip to the pub."

"Nor me," I agreed.

So between us we cooked up a story to tempt our Spartan leader out of the mountains and into the local pub. Our story was simple: we invented three girls we had met in the village. These three imaginary girls had agreed to meet us in the local pub at around 7pm.

Back at the camp, Alan was waving a tin plate, coaxing a fire into life. He greeted us, "Did you get all the stuff?"

"Yes, and we've got some good news."

"Yeah," Ray backed me up, "we met three girls in the village. They're from Sheffield University."

"What are they like?" Alan asked. "They're not bloody climbers, are they?"

"No, they're tidy, the red-haired one ain't bad," I said, "the blonde is an absolute stunner, a real corker, and the brunette… well she's quite nice if she didn't wear glasses."

We had decided not to make our descriptions too gushing or Al would smell a rat; in fact, we rehearsed our story so well, we practically began to believe the story ourselves.

At half five, Alan scaled down to the pool and dipped his head in the ice-cold water. He then produced a comb and slicked his hair. Back to the tent, where he pulled out his rucksack and from the bottom produced a pair of pristine khaki drill trousers.

With clean trousers and his hair combed, he strode out

with great purpose, saying, "What's this blonde like, then?" He was visualising and thinking the blonde was as good as his.

Ray and I lingered behind, sheepishly chatting. We both agreed Alan would kill us if he knew we had made the whole thing up. Ray said, "He'll never know, so relax."

When we were at last on the road, our steps quickened at the thought of a pint while Alan's mind was full of the prospect of meeting the blonde.

The three of us approached the Cwellyn Arms. There were a few climbing types sitting on the stone wall opposite the pub. There were no women. We entered the dark interior of the pub and there were no girls in sight; only the woman behind the bar. She had dark, deep, brooding Celtic eyes, an ample figure, and large, melon-like breasts.

A scowling Alan said, "Where's these bloody women; you know, the blonde and the other two you described?"

"Well, it inner our fault they anner turned up," Ray stuttered.

I tried to add support to him, "Bloody women, you canner trust the buggers. Anyway, we may as well have a pint while we're here," I suggested

"You buggers didn't make this all up, did you?" Alan accused.

"Don't be bloody daft, why would we?" Ray said.

"So you could have a pint. I know you buggers of old," he complained.

Back at the camp, we used the primus to heat Heinz tomato soup, slurped it down, and hit the sleeping bags.

A long climb and a missing German

Alan decreed that the next day should be devoted to some serious climbing.

We descended at speed, running side to side, zig-zagging down a long scree slope to the east of the Snowdon summit. From there, we made our way to the foot of Y Lliwedd to tackle one of its longer, challenging routes.

Thankfully, it was a sunny day when we set off. The rock was invitingly hard and dry. We stopped two-thirds of the way up and sat on a grass ledge no bigger than a paving slab. Looking back down the way we had come, the exposure was heightened. Inquisitive sea gulls flew opposite us.

We sat eating our butties and threw our crusts to the gulls, who dropped at speed down the rock face, catching up with the food. As I watched those birds fall like stones, it gave me an odd feeling, like I was being drawn down with them. I was glad when we decided to crack on.

After our break, we took on the last section to the top of the climb. There was one very tricky pitch. Alan as usual led and belayed at the top, as always talking us up with instructions: "Move to the right there, that's it, there's a big hand-hold, it's a stretch," and so it went on, until the three of us were safely at the top.

I was pleased to finish the climb. I think it was being exposed for such a long time that I found a bit challenging.

Ray said, "That was ace, I'm bloody starving."

I pointed out he had eaten a ruck of butties. "But it's not like real food, like a hot dinner," he said.

Alan replied, "I'm doing my special corned beef hash when we get back."

It spurred Ray on and I too lengthened my stride. Al's hash, as he called it, was one of his better culinary efforts and with a dollop of brown sauce it would go down very well.

Shortly after that, we bumped into some mountain rescue people. Apparently, a German woman had set off from the Royal Goat in Beddgelert to climb to the summit of Snowdon. "That was yesterday, and she didn't return," the big ginger bloke with skin like seasoned leather explained. He added, "We have lots of people all over the area. I wonder: A, if you've seen anything and B, if you would search an area for us."

Alan's response was immediate, getting his map out and agreeing a particular area to concentrate our search.

"Thanks lads, it'll save us. Where are you staying?"

Al said, "We're camped right in the middle of the area you want us to search, so it suits us down to the ground."

We formed a line and walked ten yards apart and searched for around two hours. There was no sign of anyone so we went back to our camp, got the fire going, and got stuck into Alan's corned beef, loads of onions, and spuds.

A good end to a good day. Ray praised Alan, "That was on the ball."

We built up the fire, made coffee, and sat nattering until the light slipped into darkness.

We were woken in the early hours by the tent shuddering, as if it was about to take off. Once outside, Ray put two extra guy ropes on the tent to hold it in place. Down the valley, a huge, dense, blue-black cloud was casting big shadows skittering across the landscape, weeping blankets of rain.

We secured the tents and battled through the rain, which was persisting down and becoming heavier.

"Where are we going?" I questioned Alan.

But through the rain, which was now lashing down, I could see the old wheelhouse or whatever it was. There were lots of wooden beams and scraps of timber and one small area that offered us a degree of shelter, of 12' x 10'.

"Right," said Al, "here's the plan. The weather looks set in, so I think we should break camp and get our gear up here."

"It's not much better here," Ray said.

"It will be."

Ray and I went back to the camp. It looked like it had been through a hurricane. We re-erected the small tent, took the bigger tent down, and pulled out the groundsheet, which was not sewn in. We put some gear in the small tent and carried the rest through the soaking rain up to the wheelhouse. Alan had rebuilt parts of the wall and had lodged timbers across from wall to wall. "Got the ground sheet?" he asked.

The three of us stretched the large groundsheet over the timbers and secured it all with rocks. We placed more timbers in the opposite direction and then put sods of mossy turf to complete the roof; we also used this method to plug gaps in the walls. Ray named the system 'Sod's law'. For the bed, more criss-crossed timbers, then loads of grass sods, and finally a ground sheet, and bingo, we had a monster bed. The three of us went down to the old campsite and picked up the small tent and the rest of the gear.

We had just got back to the wheelhouse when the heavens opened. The rain came in huge spots and battered our new shelter. There was the odd leak but on the whole it withstood the storm well enough.

Al heated a tin of frankfurters on the primus and we smacked them into slices of bread with bags of mustard. We all slept in a line while the wind howled around us and the rain searched for weak spots in the roof and found a few.

At first light, I got out of my sleeping bag and stepped into my boots.

"Where are you going?" a disturbed Ray asked.

"For a piddle."

Outside, it was still blowing quite hard, but the rain had stopped. Patches of blue were being exposed as the wind blew the storm across the Snowdon Horseshoe, taking the clouds with it.

We had a couple of days' climbing from our new vantage point and, as funds were running out, talk turned to ending our stay in the mountains and getting back to reality. Ray told us he was off the next morning and that night organised his rucksack.

The next morning, after fried bread, eggs and beans, it was time for Ray to head back south and get back to London to earn some dough.

We walked with him, following a stream, and eventually came to the A498 a mile or so from Beddgelert. All Ray had for his return journey was a three-pence piece, which we found imbedded in a bar of soap, one-and-a-half fags, and four matches. Alan had made him a cheese butty to take with him. We all shook hands then Al and I set off for Beddgelert and Ray went in the opposite direction, up the Gwynant Valley, thumbing with great enthusiasm, which he possessed in bucketfuls.

We shouted after him, "See you next week, Ray!"

Al and I walked into Beddgelert, strolling through the village over the bridge and up the road to the Royal Goat Hotel, where we ordered coffee. We asked about the German woman and were informed she had walked over the mountain and booked in at the Pen-y-Gwryd Hotel, on the opposite side. She had failed to ring the Royal Goat to tell them she wasn't returning, which naturally set alarm bells ringing.

After coffee, we made our way back to our camp and after another two days in which the rain persisted down once more, we decided it was time we joined Ray and went back to London. We had enjoyed a memorable stay in the mountains and now it was time to get back to work.

After a couple of nights with my family in Shrewsbury, it was back to the Smoke; an apt title for smoggy London in those days. This didn't please me as I was dreading going back to the bedsit in Chalk Farm and to work in Berkeley Square. I never did hear a nightingale sing, just sparrows and pigeons, and it mystified me why any self-respecting bird would want to live in smoggy London.

During heavy smog, in common with many other people, I always wore a handkerchief bandit-style and by the time I got home it was in part black. When I washed my hair, clouds of dirt and grit flowed down the washbasin plughole.

Oh, for the clean air of the mountains

The Driving Test

On the drive back from our holiday in Torquay, Pal suggested I get behind the wheel of the Vauxhall and try my hand at driving. The road was empty, straight and quiet, so I agreed to give it a go and confidently slipped in on the bench seat behind the wheel. Pal told me all about the clutch, showed me the instruments, and explained the purpose of the various levers and, most importantly, the brake.

We weaved our way up the road, going from side to side. "This isn't a bloody chicane, you're over-steering," Pal said. "Pull over, I'll take over."

In spite of that, the experience prompted me to somehow get a car and learn how to drive it. Some months later, a car came up for sale. It belonged to a man who lived at the top of our street in Shrewsbury. It was parked outside his house and it had a sign in the window which read, 'Low Mileage, good runner bargain price £70.'

I went to have a look at it and met the seller, who had seen me looking at it and had come out. He assured me, "It's a good runner, it's never let me down."

It was a Vauxhall Cresta and he explained that £70 was a bargain price. I explained the most I could scrape together was £60. We struck the deal and I was the proud owner of my first car: registration plate NAW 617.

When I told my dad, his reaction was, "But you can't bloody drive."

"Well, anybody can drive, even old Mrs Jones in the

terrace can drive, so it canner be that difficult."

My brother Tad said, "I'll teach the little bugger."

My father responded, "Well, you've only just passed the test yourself. Where is the car now?"

"It's on the street, up by the man's house."

"Well, we better go and get it, you can keep it round by the garages."

"Thanks, Dad."

The next lunchtime, Tad turned up with two L plates. He reversed the car out of the garage and tied the Ls back and front with string.

"Can we go out for a spin?" I said.

"No," was his response, "I'm playing footy. We'll go on Sunday. We'll have to get you a provisional licence as well."

On the Saturday, Tad and I set off to Atcham aerodrome. Gran and Mum both worriedly said, "Be careful, don't do anything stupid."

After two sessions on the aerodrome, Tad took me on a few country roads. He said to me, "You want to put in for your test."

"But I've only been out three times."

"Dunner worry," he said, "it takes weeks for the test to come through and you're doing ok."

So we applied for a date for my test.

In those days, a knowledge of the Highway Code only needed to be rudimentary, so that was no problem. I obtained a copy and swotted up.

Just a few days later, I was coming down the stairs when the postman called. I watched the post dropping onto the tiles and saw one envelope had my name on it. You'll never guess what it was.

You've guessed. It was the notification for my driving test for a week on Monday.

On telling my brother, he said, "Dunner panic, I'll take you out on the Sunday prior to your test on Monday."

"Should I try and cancel?"

"No, you'll be ok, dunner worry."

"Yes," I said, "but I will have only been out four times."

"Look at my mate Pete, he failed and he had bags of lessons."

"Well, how did he fail?"

Pete had taken his test in a firm's van where he was an apprentice. For his hill start, he was taken to Howards Bank; a fierce slope leading up to Shrewsbury Prison. The examiner told Pete to stop. He reached down for the handbrake and found there was no lever.

"Bloody hell they've given me the van with no lever," he complained and then told the examiner, "there's a brick under your seat, can you put it under the back wheel?"

The examiner failed him on the spot.

Tad said, "Of course he failed, but you've got a lever, and a brake, so dunner worry."

I supplied, "Then there was Tony Weaver had it bad an' all."

"Why?"

"He was having a test for his scooter the examiner sent him on a circuit around the Abbey, telling him he would step out with raised hand somewhere along a certain stretch. When he stepped out, Tony didn't stop, putting the examiner in hospital."

Tad sarcastically said, "I suppose they failed him!"

After my final lesson on the Sunday, Tad took me to the test centre and I went in, sat down nervously, and waited for my examiner.

He appeared on the steps, complete with clipboard, and gave me my first instruction. "Please read me the number of that car down there."

He was a little bald, miserable man, with thick glasses. I wondered if he could read the number himself. I started and have to admit I struggled to see the first letter. I stuttered, "Is it, er, er… an F?"

He interrupted, "Which car are you looking at?"

"The red one on the left."

"No, no, no," he said, "the silver one."

The silver one presented no problem and I rattled off the letters and numbers.

When we got to my car I got in, and he walked around, holding his clipboard and examining the car. He got in and adjusted his seat.

"Proceed and turn to the right," he ordered in a military sort of way.

I let the clutch out. My knee was almost in my chest before it engaged.

'So far, so good,' I thought.

By now, my back was wet with sweat as we proceeded up the Foregate, past Lord Hill's column and into Wenlock Road.

He said, "When I bang my newspaper on top of the dash, I want you to stop, as quickly as you can but still controlling the car."

This was the emergency stop my brother had warned me to expect.

I was alert and ready. When he hit the dash, I hit the brakes. However, I missed the clutch and hit the brake so hard that I locked the wheels and we went broadside onto the wrong side of the road.

He nervously said, "Proceed."

My reply was probably not a good idea. I said, "Ok, which way?" as the car was now facing slightly in the direction we had just come from.

The whole test was all like being in a dream. The one part I got right was the hill start on Wyle Cop. In fact, because of traffic, I did at least three hill starts.

The three-point-turn ended up as a four-point-turn and I mounted the pavement, or it would have been at least five or six.

I had my window open and decided it would show confidence if I drove like my father, with his elbow in fresh air and the other on the wheel.

The bald examiner snapped, "Both hands on the wheel."

He obviously hadn't seen my dad driving, but I didn't argue.

At one stage, the examiner asked me to pull over and stop. Then told me to proceed again. There was a milk float in front of me, which was hardly moving.

I looked in my mirror and overtook it. However, as I did so, there was a bump.

He said, "You clipped that vehicle."

"I did not," I said, "that was my golf clubs falling over in the boot."

He asserted, "You hit it."

"I didn't." But I pulled over to stop.

He then said, "What are you doing now?"

"If I hit the milk float, which I didn't, I'm giving my details to the milkman."

"Proceed!" he shouted. He then instructed me to turn left but I carried on. He said, louder, "I asked you to turn left."

"I know, but you were too late," I informed him.

"Take the next left, I'll be late for my next appointment."

Back at the test centre, his anger was apparent. He looked ready to boil over. He said, "Pull in at the end."

This would leave me on a bend and I knew this was wrong; you should not park on a bend, it was in the Code. There was one space which wasn't on a bend, so I decided to reverse into that.

Red-faced, he exploded, "What are you doing now?"

"I'm parking my car," I said.

He said, "I told you, on the end."

"Well, that's on a bend and everybody knows you dunner park on a bend."

In the end, knowing I had failed, I said, "Look here, mate, this is my car and it's going in that space."

I reversed perfectly, without touching the pavement. Aside from the hill start, it was the only thing I got right all day.

He scribbled on his clipboard and I asked, "I suppose I've failed?"

His reply was instant. "You most certainly have." He handed me a slip of paper with crosses top to bottom and raged off towards the test centre. You could see his anger and the steam rising off him as he strode away.

He could have given me a point for completing the course, and for my parking ability.

My brother turned up to take me and my car back to the garage.

"How did you get on, our kid?" he asked.

"Failed everything," I said.

He replied, "I'm not surprised, I would not like to take a test in that car. You've only got three forward gears and that clutch is a nightmare. Go to a driving school, you'll see what I mean. Their cars are much easier to manage."

"I just hope I dunner get the same examiner, we didn't really hit it off."

I only took a couple of weeks to get over my experience and as Tad suggested, I went to a driving school in Shrewsbury. My instructor, Mr Marsden, was a kind, older man.

The car was a Vauxhall Viva and driving it was a doddle; after my car, it was like being in charge of a roller skate.

My first lesson encompassed a drive out of town. It was a dry day so I didn't have to operate the windscreen wipers. One less thing to worry about.

On a straight piece of road, he told me to put my foot down. Then when we came to a village, he said, "Reduce your speed."

I got the message immediately. Dropping back to 30mph seemed to give me lots of time. After lots of lessons, Mr Marsden said, "You're ready, I think we can apply for a test."

I put this down to having learned a lot more from Mr Marsden. I realised all the things that can go wrong.

As I sat in the waiting area at the test centre, I was dreading that I might get the same examiner. Dead on time, the man came into the room, saying, "Roderick Shaw." What a relief – he was a small man with a friendly smile; not the tense, angry chap who did my first test.

However, in fairness to the first examiner, when I look back, his bad-tempered disposition was no doubt down to my bad driving.

During my test, after a stop and his instruction to proceed, I set off and the car shuddered, but by pressing the accelerator I managed to keep it going without stalling. I had set off in too high a gear. But maybe my mistake actually helped me pass, because I hadn't panicked.

Back at the test centre, I could see over his shoulder and there were a lot of ticks. He then asked me questions from the Highway Code, which I managed to successfully negotiate.

The ones that I struggled with went as follows:

"What is a box junction?"
As there were none in Shrewsbury at that time I answered, "I don't know."

"What is the sign for a box junction?"
I answered, "Well if I don't know what it is, I wouldn't recognise the sign."
He said, "Er, I suppose not."

"What would you do if you broke down on a motorway?"
I answered, "Well I'd get onto the hard shoulder and then get my passengers out of harm's way on the embankment."
He posed the question, "What would you do then?"
I answered, "Well, I'd phone for help."
"What is the sign for a telephone on a motorway?"
"I haven't a clue, but it would be a very good sign if you couldn't recognise it, would it?"
"Mm, I suppose not."

Throughout the test, the sweat poured down my back and was by now in floods. The examiner handed me a piece of paper with lots of ticks and said, "Well, young man, your knowledge of the Highway Code is abysmal, but your driving was well up to the mark, so I am passing you. Well done, and do a bit more reading of your highway code."

I suppressed a strong desire to hug him and instead said, "Thank you very much," and shook his hand.

He left the car and I sat there totally stunned, a gormless broad smile and a bubbling wave of pride and relief. At last, I had wheels and the freedom of the open road.

My brother turned up, opened the passenger door and asked, "Well?"

"I only went and passed!" I exclaimed.

"Well done, our kid," he said, and shook my hand.

www.ingramcontent.com/pod-product-compliance
Lightning Source LLC
Chambersburg PA
CBHW021437080526
44588CB00009B/563